WHAT THEY ARE SAYING

"Alexis Ware is an amazing person of great resolve. I love the way she communicates her passion, in this book, to overcome any obstacle to create incredible outcomes for herself and anyone fortunate enough to be in her path. Her willingness to follow God's voice and her contributions to His Kingdom are a blessing to so many including me. I am so honored to have played a small role in her journey and I am so proud of all she is about. "

Marsha Sharp, Texas Tech College Basketball Coach

"I've known Alexis Ware a long time. So let me say it: 'She's the real deal!' Over the years I've come to admire her passion for serving Jesus, her courage and obedience in following Him (including writing this book), and her impact on the lives of so many. *THE COACH'S VOICE* is the story of how Alexis, with God's help, got to be the Christian leader she is today. There are a host of spiritual takeaways within its pages that you, as a reader, will be able to draw from to inspire and encourage your own life with. That's why I highly recommend it!"

Dr. Robert Lewis, Pastor, author, and founder of Men's Fraternity

"Loving this book! So, proud of you! Every parent of a young basketball player should buy this book!

It's funny, yet so very telling of what young athletes experience...the self-doubt, necessary ego-shedding, the hard work, the trust in your coach and finally the fulfillment of your dreams! But most importantly, trusting in God that He, our Divine Creator, has this wonderful life-plan paved out for each one of His wonderful creations! All you have to do is submit to His will, and follow His path, and you will fulfill His plans for you! And, live in peace, happiness, and abundance! And, best yet, inherit, as a Child of God, and His son, Jesus Christ, the Kingdom of God!" Alexis, you are a great "fisher of men" in spreading the 'Good News' of the Gospel! Love you, so much!"

Jan Lahodny, Victoria High School Basketball Coach

"I was in the midst of organizing an event for students in Warren, Arkansas called 'Raising the Bar.' The hope was to encourage these kids, many of them coming from disadvantaged backgrounds, to aim higher in five key areas, one of which was sexual purity. I had speakers for the other four but the purity talk was the big one. A mutual friend said I should call Alexis. Who? Never heard of her. I thought I knew everybody! I'm such an idiot.

She was amazing. Her message was captivating and her delivery polished, passionate and flawless. It was one of if not the best talk on sexual purity I have ever heard.

This book is an extension of that.

Equal parts memoir and Bible study you'll get the background on the lessons Alexis has learned in her amazing life. Like a good point guard should Alexis steers you through the struggles and the triumphs, the victories and the failures in her typical raw and direct style that is sure to keep you turning the page.

I know this book will inspire you to dream big, to stand firm and to raise the bar in your pursuit of the life God has for each and every one of you."

Matt Mosler, Pastor, New Life Church, Pine Bluff, AR

"The hand of God in every aspect of Alexis Ware's life is undeniable when reading her story. The Lord brought many different people into her life, stepping in to speak truth and believing the Lord had great plans for her, at the exact time when she needed to hear truth which has grown into a faith without boundaries! I finish this book encouraged by Alexis' pursuit to live each day wholly devoted and dependent upon Christ. Her testimony is one of trust and faith, fully reliant upon the Father!"

Lacey Caldwell, Lessons for Life Board President

"You don't meet many people as open, authentic, and real as Alexis Ware. She is a dynamic personality who has penned her journey of life transformation through the matchless grace of God. You will be encouraged and inspired! Alexis makes a great assist in *THE COACH'S VOICE*. I know you will enjoy her story and all its life lessons!"

Stephan Moore, Executive Director, Shiloh Camp

"This book will empower and encourage everyone who reads it! As I was reading Alexis's stories of triumph and failure, it made me feel as if I could do all that God has called me to do during the unchallenging and challenging times of life. Alexis's willingness to be transparent and honest about her life's story, is so refreshing. This book allows you to see the Hope of Glory, Jesus Christ, in action in her life. It gives you hope as you read because you know if God did it for her, He will do it for you. "

Stephanie Fitzgerald, Field staff, Freedom in Christ Ministries

c. 1988. Alexis Ware, Point Guard, NCAA Division 1, Texas Tech Lady Raiders

The Coach's Voice

LISTENING FOR THE QUIET VOICE OF GOD

Alexis Ware

with Carol Martin

Foreword by Robert Lewis

Lessons For Life
Little Rock, Arkansas

Lessons For Life
P.O. Box 23881
Little Rock, AR 72221
(501) 590-7824
https://lessonsforlife.us/

Publisher's Cataloging-in-Publication data

Names: Ware, Alexis, author. | Martin, Carol, 1945-, author.
Title: The coach's voice : listening for the quiet voice of God / by Alexis Ware; with Carol Martin
Description: Little Rock, AR: Lessons For Life 2021.
Identifiers: ISBN: 978-1-7373010-0-4 (paperback) | 978-1-7373010-1-1 (ebook)
Subjects: LCSH Ware, Alexis. | Basketball players--United States--Biography. | Women basketball players--United States--Biography. | Christian biography. | BISAC BIOGRAPHY & AUTOBIOGRAPHY / Personal Memoirs | BIOGRAPHY & AUTOBIOGRAPHY / Sports | BIOGRAPHY & AUTOBIOGRAPHY / Religious
Classification: LCC GV886 .W367 W37 2021 | DDC 796.323/8092--dc23

Contents

"LISTEN AND HEAR MY VOICE;
PAY ATTENTION AND HEAR WHAT I SAY."
ISAIAH 28:23

I dedicate this book...

To Mom and Pops, I thank you for supporting all of my life activities. Thank you for loving me unconditionally and making limitless sacrifices. There is no way I could thank you enough for the stability that you provided for your children and all your hard work. God used you to raise me into becoming the person that I am today. You are my world and I love you dearly.

And to my siblings, James, Gwen, Pat, Vanice, LaReese and E.J., for all those times we were able to gather together and just spend time laughing and sharing our childhood memories. You have gone above and beyond to embrace my call to ministry and all that I have been able to experience. I could not have asked for better siblings. I love you dearly.

By the way, "We are ALL Mom's favorite."

Alexis Ware

2018. Left to right: Vanice, EJ, Alexis, James, Gwen, LaReese, Pat. Seated: Doris Brown (Mom)

FOREWORD

There are some people you just connect with. Instantaneously. Call it what you will, there's something about that person that resonates with you. Deeply, emotionally. They immediately feel like an old friend, but in some ways, even closer. There's a mystical, spiritual bond here. An eternal alignment.

That's how I felt when I first met Alexis Ware. We had coffee together at a local breakfast spot and she was wanting to introduce herself and her fledgling ministry, "Lessons for Life." She was a bit nervous as we started talking. But her warm face made it easy to listen. She obviously had a spiritual intensity and passion about her that was engaging. By the end of our time together, she had me completely on board. Here was someone I knew was a difference maker and would be a lifelong friend.

Since that time, I've had many other opportunities to meet with Alexis and deepen our relationship. I've listened to her as she's shared her life, her faith walk with God, her ministry challenges and setbacks, her next year's goals, and her personal dreams, one of which, years ago now, was the dream of writing this book. When she first mentioned her book idea to me at one of our coffees, she quickly expressed how intimidating that task felt.

"How do you even begin?" she laughed.

I've learned with Alexis, a lot in her life begins with "a call." From an inward urging. A spiritual prompting. More than most she has a keen sense of God's direction along with the courage to obey. It was a call that led Alexis to join Athletes in Action after college. It was a call that pushed her to move into the STEP inner city ministry. It was a call that led her to help at a local church's Care Center. It was a call that pushed her on stage to publicly address students on critical life issues such as sexual purity, and then, in an even bolder step, to start the Lessons for Life mentoring program as a single woman that she leads to this day. So when Alexis said about writing a book, "How do you even begin?", I should have said, "Alexis, if God is calling you to write a book, it will only be a matter of time until it happens."

Being led by God is the Alexis Ware story. That's why *The Coach's Voice* is the perfect title. It's not that there haven't been missteps and failures along the way. There have been. Alexis's life, as with all of us, is far from perfect. But her story, flaws and all, is an upward story. It's one of a believing person grasping for God's best, holding on and obeying even when it's hard to do so, persevering through hard times, and trusting in God's values against a compromised culture. In it all, Alexis's life is one of real life faithfulness and of God coming through.

I'm a better person for having met Alexis. I believe you'll be a better person for having read her story!

Robert Lewis
Pastor, Author, Founder - Men's Fraternity, BetterMan
June 30,2021

INTRODUCTION

I WANT YOU

"If they want you, they'll have to send for you!" mom said irritably.

Texas Tech told my family that they'd also offer my sister, Gwen, a scholarship if I signed with them. We'd both go on full basketball scholarships. My parents were ecstatic. However, after I accepted the scholarship, they called back and said Gwen's grades would not transfer, therefore, she would not be eligible for a scholarship. My mom was disappointed, angry, thinking they'd set me up. She insisted I refuse to go there. I never went against my parents' wishes, but this time I did. I intended to go to Texas Tech and play basketball for the Lady Raiders.

Mom conceded enough to pay for my ticket and drive me to the bus station, but she wouldn't drive me to the campus. After exchanging some "I love yous" and hugs, we parted, and I boarded the bus to take my seat close to the driver. For the first time in my life, I was very much alone.

Texas Tech, located in Lubbock, Texas, was 500 miles away from Victoria, Texas. In the fall of 1986, alone and inexperienced, I rode a bus eighteen hours with total strangers, leaving my family behind. Sadness overwhelmed me. As the bus moved away from the station, tears welled up, and loneliness overwhelmed me. All the support and love my family gave me was in the back window, growing smaller.

The bus trip was long because it made lots of stops. I'd never ridden a bus like this before, so every stop alarmed me, wondering if it was my stop. The driver assured me he'd let me know. This was one of the scariest things I'd ever done.

When I arrived in Lubbock, the assistant coach, Jane't Howey, met me at the bus station and loaded up all my boxes. She took me to the dorm and helped me unload, before leaving me with strangers. My roommate wasn't there yet, so I was alone, wondering what was next. Unpacking my clothes gave a little relief from the fears, but the campus and dorm were new and unknown. I realized the recreation center was just across the street, so I walked over and played basketball with other students. Basketball, at least, was something familiar.

The rest is history. That was the beginning of a basketball college career which led to competing at the highest level with the Texas Tech Lady Raiders team in NCAA Division 1.

But this story isn't just about basketball. Self-doubt has haunted me and defined every stage of my life. This is the story of a journey from insecurity to confidence, fear to freedom. It began with trusting a high school basketball coach but led to a lifetime of trusting my Savior, taking me across the globe.

True freedom came to me in increments as I exposed myself to God's Word, His ways and His people. Along the way many fears were replaced with grace and freedom. After leaving home, I discovered that the world's freedom and God's freedom were two different things. This is the story of my journey, God's molding of who I am, and the freedom found on the other side of obedience.

This book isn't about me either. Instead, it's about God and the journey He takes us on with Him.

CHAPTER 1

HIGH SCHOOL BASKETBALL

POINT GUARD POTENTIAL

“You’re on a camping trip and have to go to the bathroom in the woods,” Coach Jan Lahodny said as she paced back and forth in front of the Victoria High School girls’ basketball team. The Victoria Stingerettes had won three state championships in the past under the leadership of Coach Lahodny. South Texas knew the Stingerettes well, and we were the team to beat.

“Show me how low you’d squat. Freeze. To play defense, that’s how low you must go. Now hold that position, dragging your fingers along the sideline of the basketball court. I’m timing you for five minutes. Get ready. Go!”

I looked at the rest of the girls, puzzled, wondering if Coach had lost her mind. However, I soon realized she was dead serious. We squatted and shuffled around the court. Two minutes into this exercise my legs burned, and I was in tremendous pain. Tears formed, but I pushed through and completed that grueling drill. At the end I wanted to lie down on the court and pass out, but there were more drills to come which were just as painful and strenuous. Because the team trusted Coach, we did it all, even when I didn’t know the purpose of a drill. The drills always developed something in me that I needed for the game. That fall of 1982, my freshman year, I could hardly wait to wear the red and white high school basketball uniform of the Victoria Stingerettes.

Those practicing with the team weren't random players. Coach Lahodny had been watching players, from the two local middle schools, Crain Middle School and Howell Middle School. She trained the middle school coaches to use plays she used with her high school team. Because she hated wasting time, Coach wanted middle school basketball players to learn the plays she'd implement in high school. That kind of forward thinking strategy prepared us for success. When we reached high school, we already knew the fundamentals of her style of basketball and were ready for more intense and specific training.

In 7th grade, my 8th-grade-sister Gwen already played basketball. Basketball was never on my radar, and I'd never even shot a basketball. Because Gwen was a talented player, the middle school coach expected me to be the same. I knew I was an unskilled player, so when I made the team, I assumed it was because of my sister's talent. How could I ever measure up to her?

I worried that they really didn't want me on the team. I'd never be good enough. My insecurity told me everyone was looking at me and thinking I wasn't good enough. Although my abilities were similar to everyone else's on the team, I somehow put myself lower. As a result, I played basketball timidly. When I missed a basket, I hesitated to take another shot. Because I knew my dribbling skills weren't up to par, I quickly passed the ball to the nearest teammate.

EARLY DAYS

Growing up in a big family in Victoria, Texas, it wasn't easy to claim attention. I was third out of seven, so I didn't think I had a voice. I suspected whatever I had to say wasn't important. Every sibling held a different position in the family unit. My position was peacemaker. If there was a conflict, I always followed behind to smooth things out. Any kind of trouble unnerved me. For example, if my parents had an argument, anxiety could overtake me. My heart beat hard and my mind raced, as I quickly sought to turn the tide, usually by trying to distract everyone's attention away from the situation. A quick peace was my objective.

Maybe that's why at school I quickly became the class clown. I loved making people laugh, but to get that reward, I had needed to get really loud, so everyone heard my amusing and clever comments. The laughter was worth the punishment. Eventually, I realized that I was the only student being sent to the principal's office. The teachers weren't entertained by my impulsive, attention-seeking humor. I was the poster child for this verse:

"The mouths of fools are their undoing." Proverbs 18:7a.

In middle school, my disrespect for authority and my demand to do things my way went unchecked. Some days during warm up for a basketball game, I set a chair on the free throw line and shot balls sitting down. The other girls retrieved them for me. No one ever called me out for doing such an outrageous thing. I'd worn everyone down and did my own thing so often that they gave up trying to tell me anything. The defiance and silliness covered up my feelings of inadequacy and worthlessness.

Because I was cutting up in class and on the court, the middle school coaches wanted to drop me from the team. However, even in middle school, Coach Lahodny saw potential in me.

She assured everyone, "You don't kick talent off the team! There's no way Alexis Ware will be cut, and I'll guarantee she'll get it together."

Because of her intervention, I survived middle school basketball and joined the 9th grade team.

Earning my red and white Victoria Stingerette uniform wasn't easy. Players weren't just handed a high school uniform. We needed to earn it, piece by piece. We practiced drills that built up defensive footwork and shooting, while incorporating conditioning. Because my skills were improving, I knew I could be successful at the drills. Some drills were for individuals while others required group effort. If even one player failed during a group drill, the whole team went back to square one and started over.

It was easy to earn the shoes and jersey, but the shorts and leggings were harder. Often, someone played in a basketball game with odd-colored shorts or leggings because she hadn't earned her uniform items yet. Determined, I fought through the painful drills. In my mind, playing with an incomplete uniform was shameful. Earning my uniform was my main motivation to work hard and meet all the requirements. Fortunately, I was blessed and never played a game without a complete uniform.

Surprisingly, a written test covered our newly learned skills. Because academics weren't important to me and I usually just got by, taking a written test made me freeze in fear. Although I knew basketball, I feared that I couldn't express it on paper. In my mind, I had to score well, or Coach might think I didn't know the game of basketball. On test day, I entered the gym, heart pounding, insecure, so afraid of disappointing Coach. We all sat on the gym floor as she passed out the test.

I leaned over to write. I read question one. I knew the answer!

Question two: I knew that one, too!

My pounding heart settled down as I went through the test. After answering the last question, I turned in my paper. The test was graded immediately, and I'd scored extremely high. Sighing with relief, I proudly walked out of the gym, head held high.

Because Coach pulled from two middle schools, she knew her team had the potential to dominate conference play. Our team was strong, and that year, we won most games. During my freshman year, I learned to love the game and my basketball IQ increased. However, it was still unclear what position I'd play on the high school team, because my talent was undeveloped.

At the end of 1983, my 9th grade year, Coach Lahodny spoke life-changing words, "I want you to play point guard on varsity next year."

That was my high school basketball coach talking—or was it God?

Breathless in shock, I knew I was not good enough.

My basketball skills weren't strong enough to play on the championship-winning varsity team. Playing point guard would put tremendous pressure on me because the point guard position is like being a coach on the floor, talking and directing teammates. If I didn't understand the whole game, how could I lead the team? Was I as valuable as the coach thought? What would my teammates think? They knew I wasn't skilled. Would they make fun of me? Suddenly, insecurity overtook me.

"What?" I was shocked.

"I said, next year I want you to be my starting point guard."

"I don't even know how to dribble," I said. "And I can't shoot." I shook my head and waved my hands palms up, questioning my own abilities. Impossible!

"I'll teach you to dribble and shoot. Trust me, I will teach you everything you need to know," she said confidently.

In those few words, I heard, "I promise to spend time with you, invest in you, develop skills in you."

Although Coach understood my weaknesses, she also saw talent in me and agreed to take me to a different place. This would be a lot of work. Varsity was serious, and expectations were higher. Could I do this?

I was astonished that Coach Lahodny wanted me to be a starting player on the varsity team as point guard, a crucial position. Coach's expectations and fans' expectations were at stake. How could I do this as a sophomore, when normally this would be an upper classman position?

I'd need to listen to the coach, and the team's job was to listen to me. For once, my loudness was an asset.

Coach's request brought out insecurities I didn't know I had. To battle those insecurities, I overcompensated by spending every waking hour that summer practicing basketball skills. She gave me a list of drills, so I responded with determination and commitment. She showed me how to slow down and get ready to shoot. I needed to reposition my hands, adjust my stance and balance, and then shoot. The summer before my sophomore year, I dribbled and shot the basketball everywhere I went. Even when I walked the neighborhood with my mom and her friends, I dribbled. Coach told me to dribble two basketballs at once on pea gravel, which was tricky because of the uneven surfaces. That skill would make it easier to dribble on the court. Would all that work be enough?

Finally, I decided to trust Coach, even though I didn't see success as possible.

Hesitatingly, I told her, "Well, okay."

That was the beginning of a basketball career which led to competing at the highest level with the Texas Tech Lady Raiders team in NCAA Division 1A. I faced my sophomore high school basketball season with self-doubt and insecurity.

I wanted to be point guard. I spent every waking hour that summer practicing with Coach's list of drills. It was a summer of determination and commitment. When I returned to school in the fall, I stunned everyone—including myself—with my progress. Watching me practice, Coach often pulled me aside for additional instructions. Her confidence in her coaching built confidence in me. Her words carried power, and I treasured the individual attention.

As a point guard, my loud voice was a positive asset because the team could hear me shout commands. The point guard position isn't the "ball hog" of the team. That's a self-centered player who's only concerned with her own personal glory or her own statistics for scoring, rebounding and playing time. Instead, the point guard is a team player, motivated by a team win, without regard for her own glory. Coach recognized that I wanted to win but didn't have to take the credit. Instead, I could pull the team together, motivate and encourage them.

Coach was also a mentor to the whole team. We were a family, she taught, so if one of us hurt, we all hurt. If someone did well, we all did well. To support that attitude, the starting lineup was chosen by the team. Before a game, each teammate passed in her own list for the starting lineup, so no one could accuse the coach of playing favorites. They chose me to start all but one game. That one game caused me to run down the road of defeat and self-questioning again. My fragile confidence shattered. At my core, I was still insecure. But Coach leaned over and assured me everything was okay. A minute after that game started, she put me in.

By the middle of the 10th grade, scouts from Texas Tech were already recruiting me. My only interest in Tech was the possibility of meeting some fine guys. By my junior year of high school, I knew my value as a basketball player. Often, I aggressively stole the ball. I could score, but I didn't have to score. The good of the team overrode my desire to have personal recognition. I had become a strong point guard.

AWAKENING

"If you were the only person in the world, Jesus would have died for you!"

When I first heard those words, I was sitting in a Fellowship of Christian Athletes (FCA) gathering, led by Mona Garrett, the volunteer ministry leader of FCA at Victoria High School. Because Coach Lahodny had suggested I attend the weekly high school FCA meeting, I went.

Mona's words stunned me. I couldn't comprehend anyone dying for ME, especially in the light of my negative behavior. Yet, there were those words. "If you were the only person in the world, Jesus would have died for you!"

As a child, I attended church often, but somehow, I missed the message of salvation. Although I considered myself a spiritual person, church was just something you did on Sundays. I was a moral young lady mostly because I wanted to please my parents. I heard Jesus was real, that He loved me, He gave His life for me, but I always held Him at arm's length. He was "out there," but not close. He was not part of my daily life.

Mona Garrett's words made me realize Jesus wanted a relationship with ME. Something stirred in my sixteen-year-old heart, and I realized my need for Him. I had done nothing to deserve His sacrifice for me, yet He did it anyway. Mona's words said so. She asked us to raise our hands if we wanted to accept Christ as our Savior. Looking around, the whole room seemed to raise their hands, and I didn't want to be left out, so I raised my hand, too. Although it seemed like the thing to do, I responded to as much of the gospel as I could understand. I believed Jesus saved me from hell, and He was my Savior. This was a fragile beginning, but a beginning, nonetheless.

Through FCA, I began to establish personal spiritual disciplines that I still have today. Mona Garrett, met with us weekly and gave us a book, Survival Kit: Five Keys to Spiritual Growth by Ralph W. Neighbor, Jr. Through it, I learned how to have a quiet time, a daily pattern including the components of prayer, Bible reading and scripture memory.

Mona Garrett also sent individual letters of encouragement, and sometimes, a team letter to be read before a game. She was showing us the Christian faith in the real world. These letters were treasures to me personally. Always, she enlarged our understanding of our scope of influence to include those who would come behind us.

In one letter, she said, "You leave behind a tremendous example for those following in your steps."

She pointed us to a bigger picture. "Put first things first and that is Christ. Each of you are born-again Christians, which gives you the greatest source of power in all you do...Girls, read and study your Bible. Make it not only a daily routine, but a habit. Be very firm and know what you believe. That is, know right from wrong, defined so well that you won't have to ponder the answer...if you do, then probably the peer pressure won't cause you to make the wrong decision...you'll never be free from temptation. I challenge you to be strong...believe me, you'll never be sorry for saying, 'No thank you!'"

She helped us understand that basketball was more than the next game, the next victory, the next award. It carried with it a forward momentum bigger than us and the present moment.

For years, I believed lies about myself: I couldn't do things, I wasn't smart enough, I wasn't capable, I didn't fit in, or I didn't have purpose. Between Coach, Mona Garrett, and a new understanding of Jesus, I began to strike down those lies, one by one.

Coach's faith showed us how to live devoted to Christ. She connected basketball with a life in Christ, and we responded. For the next three years, Coach prayed with us before and after each game, win or lose. And sometimes even midgame. We always invited our opponents to join us in prayer after a game, and we stood with them hand-in-hand praying in center court. We learned humility when we joined hands with a team who had just beat us. Through the example of these women, basketball, and FCA, I was connecting Jesus with my life. Somehow the two needed to go together.

OLD HABITS

"I don't want to hear it! Go to the office!" Although her voice was low, cold and stern, Coach's countenance screamed disappointment. Before I could offer excuses, she gave me "the look."

I was face-to-face with the only person I allowed to have authority over me at school. Coach's coldness coupled with her very few words, caused fear and anxiety to run through my whole body. Her disappointment hurt worse than any punishment I might get. After this, she might care for me less. I wished I hadn't gone to school that day, but I did and now I was in big trouble.

The trouble began at a school assembly. Before the program started, a classmate sitting next to me began to laugh—a loud, cackling laugh, that drew everyone's attention. When she stopped, I told her to do it again, but this time sit right behind me. She scooted over and hid in back of me, while I imitated her with exaggerated movements. Everyone around thought it was me making the noise, and they all laughed hysterically. It didn't take long for one of the principals to spot the noise and give me all the credit. He looked directly at me, maintained eye contact and motioned for me to come to the gym floor. As I walked down the bleachers, everyone stared. I was self-conscious, but I wasn't afraid. Previous consequences had always been harmless and brought me even more attention. This time, however, when I reached the gym floor, I knew I was doomed. Up till now, Coach had only heard about my outrageous behavior. Because her office was right off the gym, I instantly knew she had watched the whole thing and was seeing my behavior firsthand. My reputation was catching up with me.

With deep sadness, I turned and walked to the office alone. I knew I was in trouble, but didn't know what kind of trouble. The principal told me I couldn't attend the rest of the assembly, and I'd be in lunch detention the next day. No big deal, I thought.

Thinking I was off the hook, I showed up for basketball practice in 4th period. Assuming Coach would punish me by making me run, I was all prepared mentally for that. However, when I walked into the gym Coach approached me and briefly looked up at me. Sounds of rubber bouncing off wood filled the whole gym, but when Coach came to me, all bouncing stopped. The girls on the team were pretending to be disinterested, but everyone was waiting to see what she would do to me.

In a quiet emotionless voice she said, "You aren't allowed to practice with the team for one week. You will go to the library during 4th period and write a report on how to be respectful during an assembly."

Her lack of warmth killed me. I had disappointed her. My heart sank.

Then, she turned her back on me and walked away.

In the quiet gym, the team stared at me as I slowly strode off court. Because we considered ourselves to be a family, I realized I had let down the whole team, as well as the coach. I was humiliated. Rejected. Devastated. Abandoned. There was no defense for what I had done, and I knew it. I had to take the consequences.

BACK IN THE DAY

I'd learned the basics of taking the consequences for my actions at home from my step-father. Several years after my parents' divorce, a wonderful man came into my mom's life and became the father to our family, which at the time consisted of my mom and five kids. Pops, as we called him, was willing to take us under his wing and provide for us. Because he worked in construction, he was muscular and strong. We only saw him at night—after he had worked a 12+ hour-day—and on weekends. We saw the strong work ethic in him, and we all have that going for us today. Finally, I had a father who wouldn't leave, a complete family. His presence brought us a new security that we needed. We knew we'd be protected, provided for, and loved by him.

Pops was extremely loyal to our family. One day he told my mom, "I love these kids as much as you love them." He wanted the best for us and expected us to be respectful to others in return.

c. 1985 Doris and Larence "Pops" Brown

A disciplinarian, Pops was the true leader in the house. One night several of my siblings and I were fighting with each other and things escalated to a loud racket. Pops arose from bed, and in an unnervingly calm voice asked us, "What are you all doing fighting this late at night?"

Silence.

"Tonight you'll clean this whole house! Maybe next time you'll think about what you're doing before you do it." His calm demeanor sobered all of us. Nobody resisted.

Deep into the night, we quietly washed walls and cleaned the baseboards. Occasionally, he joined us to check our progress. I remember him holding my index finger and running it along the baseboard, seeking dust. If we found any, he told us to start all over. When we had finished, the entire house sparkled and smelled like bleach. That was the last time any of us fought in the middle of the night like that. He'd given us a consequence we earned but didn't like. Even in his discipline, I knew he loved me. I was secure in his correction. He loved us enough to punish negative behavior.

CAUGHT AND CRUSHED

A few days after being disciplined for acting up in the assembly, I walked through the gym on my way home. Coach Lahodny stopped me and said, "A recruiter from Texas Tech was here to see you practice."

But of course, I wasn't practicing with the team that week.

Eyes bulging in disbelief and horrified, my stomach sinking, I demanded, "What did you tell them?"

"The truth," Coach said calmly. "I want them to know about your conduct since you could be joining their team. I always want colleges to recruit from me, so I must be honest. I have to tell them the truth, so they'll trust my judgement."

I was devastated, embarrassed, and afraid that my chances for playing with Texas Tech were over. This was a true wake-up call for me. Indeed, Proverbs spoke loudly to me!

> **"There is a way that appears to be right, but in the end it leads to death." Proverbs 14:12**

I had sought attention by being loud, the class clown. But now it may have killed my chances at playing college basketball, or even going to college at all.

This serious wake-up call made me realize my bad behavior would cost me my future in basketball. I came face-to-face with the penalty of my outrageous behavior. The attention I got wasn't important enough for it to take away the one thing I loved most, basketball. Looking back, I realized that this experience was life changing.

I would die without basketball. Everyday when I woke up, the first thought in my mind was basketball; every conversation I had was somehow centered around basketball; my reason to improve anything was tied to basketball. Threatening to take me out of basketball was my mother's greatest motivator.

Basketball was the one and only thing I did well, the only thing I loved. It was my identity, my security blanket. It was my world, almost an idol. Because Coach cared for me, she allowed me to experience the consequences even though it hurt her. This lesson-for-life made me realize I could choose my behavior, but I couldn't choose my consequence.

"The thief comes only to steal and kill and destroy..." John 10:10a

The path I was choosing was stealing my joy, killing my dreams and destroying my future.

CELEBRATING TOO SOON (11th Grade)

"We'll meet you at State!" We'd just lost a basketball game to Yates High School and were filing by, shaking hands with each opponent. Yet one of our players shouted this outrageous promise to them.

I looked at my teammate and said quietly, "You've lost your mind. There's no way we're going to make it to State!"

Although we had improved amazingly by our junior year in 1985, in a preseason tournament we played Yates High School, which had a reputation of playing rough. They intimidated opponents by talking smack and making aggressive moves the referee couldn't see. Their coach had humiliated our coach by bad-mouthing her and us, which offended our whole team because we loved Coach Lahodny so much. Our team was full of anxiety because we'd been told how good Yates was. They beat us before the game started. The intimidation took us out of the game mentally. It was obvious to the team and the crowd, that we wouldn't win. And we didn't. We lost by over 20 points.

Fear caused us to make poor game choices, and we all knew it. With our heads down, some even covered with towels and a few crying (me), we shuffled into the musty locker room. Sitting quietly in disheartened sadness, we all awaited Coach. There was no sound, except for occasional sniffing. When Coach entered the room, she calmly explained to us why we lost. We didn't follow through with our strategy. Even though we worked hard leading up to the game, we seemed to forget how to execute the game plan. She turned on her heel and walked out of the very silent locker room.

Shame hovered above me as I drew into myself. Beneath the towel on my head, I cried and cried. I hadn't played well enough. I displeased her. I brought shame to her and to the team. All I wanted to do was bury myself in these destructive thoughts. Even when the whole team went to a restaurant afterward, I didn't eat. Only time could override the turmoil in me.

However, during the season, our team got better and better, so we made it to the regional play-offs. One game was against San Antonio Judson High. Clarissa Davis, a six-foot-tall point guard, was their star player, and she played with an intensity we'd never seen before. She was a beast on the court and proved to be unstoppable.

Coach told us to guard her, saying, "I don't care what anyone else does, you stay with her. Face guard her."

Face guarding means Coach was telling us to stare into her eyes the whole time we were guarding her. This disrupts the offensive player's vision, whether or not they have the basketball. Or I should hold my whole hand close to, but not touching, her face to block her vision and concentration. This can totally frustrate a player.

Initially, Coach assigned me to guard her. I stood 5'6" inches against her 6'. I saw her as my very own Goliath. Initially, I was intimidated simply by her height and skills. Clarissa's job was to bring the ball down the court and start the play. As good as she was defensively, her ability to score amazed me.

Coach's strategy was to wear Clarissa out by frequently changing the player who guarded her. I understand that we needed to slow her down, even if we couldn't stop her. I only needed to do the best I could and try my hardest.

No one thought Victoria could win that game. However, we played courageously and kept the scores close. Right before the halftime buzzer, I got the ball and threw it from half court, and it went in. Everyone screamed, slapped high-fives, and celebrated. The momentum turned, and our confidence grew. Maybe, we could win. By the end, Clarissa had run out of gas. She had almost single-handedly scored Judson's points by herself, but through team effort, we persevered and took the victory.

We had a successful season (29 wins and the single loss to Yates High School), and we qualified for the state tournament held at the University of Texas in Austin. Because of so many schools in Texas, it was hard to earn the opportunity. We needed to play and win five playoff games, which included district, bidistrict, area and regional tournaments. Only four teams made it through to compete for the State Championship. Ironically, the first game we played was against Yates. Their girls were tall and muscular, and their dominance made everyone fear them. Playing them was usually a David-and-Goliath encounter. Too often, their opponents seemed defeated before the games ever began. As we had at the beginning of the season.

My first thought was, "Uh oh!"

However, I realized the Stingerettes were a much better team.

We weren't the same team Yates had beaten earlier in the season. We'd become a well-oiled machine, reading each other's minds and functioning as a unit on the court, a true team. They didn't intimidate us this time. Our winning season, encouragement from our families and coaches, and hard work built confidence into the Stingerettes.

As the game started, my teammate shouted to the Yates team, "See I told you we'd meet you at State!"

This was the most important game of the year. Coach always imparted an atmosphere of formality by choosing to show up for the games in extremely dressy clothes, complete with high heels. Her respectful demeanor underscored the importance she placed on this game. Some people even said they came to the games just to see what she was wearing. This time, she walked confidently onto the court wearing a red leather skirt, blazer and heels. Team colors.

Coach had done her homework by scouting Yate's methods, plays and strategies. After understanding Yates' style of play, coach required us to duplicate their tactics in practice, then execute a successful opposing strategy to defeat them. One tactic was to concentrate on blocking out their best rebounder to prevent them from even being able to rebound. Coach usually gave this position to our best defensive post player. Another strategy was to make sure we took care of the ball. This meant having low turnovers, making sure we didn't throw the ball away on the offensive end of the court. This required us to take higher percentage shots that ensured we were likely to score.

Different defensive looks was another strategy for our battle against Yates. This meant we'd guard them differently. Sometimes we would defend man-to-man (one-on-one), but other times we would run a trap defense (two-on-one), or maybe a zone defense (covering only a specific area). They weren't expecting these various defensive plays, and it caught them off guard. We were playing with a higher level of intensity.

Although, the game was tough, because of our successful year, the Stingerettes played with a new confidence. We scored; Yates scored; we scored again. Each time we made a basket, the Yates' player's faces registered surprise. Their confidence shrank. I thought they assumed we would give them an easy win because of their earlier season blow out with us. When the halftime buzzer sounded, the Stingerettes led. We gracefully jogged into the locker room amidst fans screaming.

We encouraged each other with, "Good job!"

"We can win this!"

"We got this!"

We quieted when Coach entered the locker room. All eyes were focused on her. This time she entered clapping her hands, applauding us. For the next few minutes, she poured praise and encouragment on us, recognizing our efforts. We were ecstatic that we had pleased Coach. She urged us to continue doing what we were doing; the strategies were working. It was as if she guaranteed us victory.

The adrenalin flowing through me, energized my thinking. Electricity filled the room. My temporary exhaustion from playing the first half so intensely left me. I was convinced we could win.

During the second half, scores went back and forth. The crowd on both sides of the court stood and screamed. Coach nervously chewed ice throughout the game. I was amazed at the quiet confidence inside me. The intensity of the game increased all the way to the buzzer. When it rang, we'd won. We screamed in victory. Jumping, hugging, high-fiving, screaming!

The Yates team fell where they stood, laid on their backs and cried in disbelief, hands covering their faces, towels over their heads. Because this was a state playoff game, their loss was even more intense.

The Victoria Stingerettes were ecstatic and ready to celebrate. Fans and family members jubilantly joined the team to eat, then followed us back to the hotel rooms. We needed to play another game the next day for the championship, but the adrenalin was flowing, and everyone wanted to keep talking about the Yates game, rejoicing in this unexpected victory.

Nobody could settle down enough to sleep, so the celebrating went long into the night. I was on cloud nine. We had worked so hard and it paid off. Shock, disbelief and excitement flooded through me.

Regrettably, we celebrated too soon.

Most of us didn't get to sleep till early morning, but had to rise before 9 a.m. for breakfast so it would settle before the game.

Later that day, as we sluggishly walked onto the court for the championship game, our exhaustion was obvious. We were out of gas before the game even started. Normally, during the warm-up time, we'd be full of adrenalin, laughing, cutting up, looking forward to the competition. However, that day, we were just going through the motions. No adrenalin at all. The Dallas South Oak Cliff team ran all over us, and we lost the game and the championship. We were disappointed, but Coach told us to hold our heads high because the Stingerettes had experienced a great season. Although we lost, and I cried again, it wasn't as deep a disappointment as when Yates tromped us. We had made it to State against all odds.

PRIDE GOES BEFORE A FALL

Basketball season was followed closely by track season. The district track meet was held at Angleton High School, Angleton, TX, and I was scheduled to run. Track meets are scored by a team accumulating points from all events. Our track coach, Norma Kremling, with Jan Lahodny assisting, had prepped the team on what each teammate needed to score in their event, in order to give us an overall victory.

Before the race, Coach said, "The best we can do is come in second."

The words sucked the life out of me. All season long we-worked hard to do well, and I didn't like the thought of it ending abruptly. My motivation was shot, and I was truly shaken. Anxiety flooded my thoughts.

"If we can't win the whole track meet, I really don't want to run," I thought. If we couldn't win, why compete? I wanted to be a winner. Losing meant I was less than a winner.

Coach Lahodny had signed me up to run the 800-meter relay, the 400-meter dash, the mile relay, the long jump, and the triple jump.

Over the three full days of track and field events, scores were added up for every team. On the last day, Coach said we were short points because some teammates hadn't placed as expected. Angleton was ahead, while we were a close second. Only one event remained, the mile relay. For this race, one team member runs a lap around the track, and then hands off a baton, a short stick, to the next, who runs their laps. I was the last runner for our team; I ran the anchor leg of the race.

Because Angleton had the second-best time in the mile relay, the only way they'd lose was if they got disqualified or if they got fourth place on the mile relay. But Angleton was expected to sweep the whole meet and become district champs.

It was a sunny spring day, and the stands were filled with excited fans. The asphalt track encircled a lush green field containing areas for long jump, triple jump, high jump, shot put, javelin, and discus.

I reconsidered my decision to not run the relay. "Many people attended this meet to watch us," I thought, "and I don't want to humiliate myself and let them think I'm not a good runner."

I decided to run, but everyone assumed we'd lose just because of our overall score. Still, I was determined to do the best I could.

I shifted nervously from one foot to the other, as I waited impatiently, watching our team's third runner race around the track, waiting for the baton hand off. Although our girls ran hard, we were losing ground. It looked like Angleton had the win.

Frustrated because we were so far behind, I shouted, "How do I run this, Coach?"

She shouted back, "Like a 100-yard dash!"

Normally, a mile relay runner is advised not to take off in a dead sprint because they must pace themselves, so they'll have enough energy to finish the race. By the time I received the baton, the Angleton runner had a half lap lead. However, I needed to run the final lap full out. I stood, adrenalin pumping, poised and in position to receive the baton. The audience was on their feet, screaming. I ran like I'd never run before, the longest sprint of my life. I chased the Angleton runner who was half a lap ahead. The distance between us shortened. Soon, I was within a couple strides of her. By the last 100 yards, we were neck-in-neck. A small bump into each other put me a step ahead of her. The finish line was getting closer and closer. In my mind, everything was in slow motion. I saw nothing but the finish line. Only a few feet from the end, the Angleton runner tripped. She fell to the ground, and the baton flew out of her hand. Although she was only a few feet from the finish line, all she had to do was pick up the baton and reach across the line for a win. But the fall rattled her, and she stumbled around.

Coach later said, "Then God sent the wind."

A gust of air mysteriously picked up the baton and blew it away from her reach. I won the race—we won the race. Bending over, trying to catch my breath, I suddenly heard the audience screaming, just going crazy. I looked up but didn't understand what was going on. I still thought that even though I won that race, we probably wouldn't win the whole meet.

Two more runners came in. By that time, the Angleton runner regained her focus, retrieved the baton and crossed the finish line in fourth place.

Coach was ecstatic, but also puzzled. Why did the Angleton runner trip? We went to the press box to watch the instant replay. What we saw astounded us. When the Angleton runner saw me gaining on her, she became angry and hit me in the head with the baton. I never felt it. Her action caused her to trip and to drop the baton. Ultimately, her confusion and that mysterious wind did the rest. Other runners passed her by. Because she finished in 4th place, Victoria High School was the 1985 District Champion!

Truly, this Philippians verse spoke loudly about staying focused on winning.

"Forgetting what is behind and straining toward what is ahead, I press on toward the goal to win the prize for which God has called me heavenward in Christ Jesus." Philippians 3:13b-14

Although this was a literal race, and the victory resulted in a trophy, I remembered this lesson at other times, when the "race" of surviving a tough time with perceived certain failure required perseverance and endurance.

By contrast, Angleton's team thought they had a sure win, so they likely entered that race with less focus. A weak commitment coupled with pride was their downfall. And, for sure, it's against the rules to hit the opponents' heads with the baton. When their runner dropped the baton, retrieving it seemed so simple; after all, it lay just a couple of feet away from the finish line. However, the runner had lost focus.

Because I always wanted the potential of being a winner, I nearly abandoned my place in this story. Running a race we could not win seemed a waste of time and effort. A sure loss diluted my motivation to even try. The anxiety I experienced at the beginning of my lap gave way to confidence, peace, and a certainty that it's not about me; it's about the team. If I'd decided not to run, my team would have never won the championship. God was also teaching me to finish what I start, even when the odds were against me.

NEW HABITS

"Alexis," Coach Lahodny said, "your name was drawn out of a hat to receive a special scholarship to attend the summer FCA (Fellowship of Christian Athletes) conference in Ft. Collins, Colorado, all expenses covered."

I don't believe she drew my name randomly. Coach had again paved the road for me to continue maturing as a basketball player and a Christian.

Regardless of how I received the free trip, I was excited that I was chosen. I had no idea what an FCA conference was about but was eager to go for two reasons: I'd never been out of Texas, and I'd never been on a college campus.

Colorado State University hosted the 1985 FCA conference. As the bus drove toward a new state, the team sang camp songs, and we had loud fun. This was my first sight of a real mountain. The massive mountains of the Colorado Rockies stunned me. What a contrast to the flatlands of South Texas! I saw dorms, classroom buildings, the library, and the recreational center on the CSU campus.

Athletic kids from all over the United States attended, and we heard motivating Christian speakers, took part in team-building activities, and attended breakout sessions. Angie Paccione, a professional women's basketball player for the Columbus Minks, was the speaker whose words pierced my heart. Standing over 6' tall, Angie spoke to us with an authority that commanded we listen closely. Because of her position as a professional athlete, I was ready to hear and believe anything she said. The auditorium was filled with several hundred excited high school students.

c. 1993. Angie Paccione and Alexis meeting eleven years later.

She challenged us to ask Jesus into our hearts, not only as our Savior but also as our Lord. Angie encouraged us to put Him first. She was speaking to hundreds of students. But for me, it was as if I was alone, hearing her words, inviting me to give up complete control. I was aware of something different, something life-changing. God was speaking to me personally through Angie, and I needed to realize for the first time, God had to become part of my every day, not just my Sunday.

The concept of LORD began to form. I understood finally that Jesus wanted to be first in my life—in every area of my life. Instead of me being my own boss, I became willing for Jesus to be my boss. As I walked into my future, daily relinquishing control of all things, big and small, I found peace and freedom in not being in control. My motives changed as I tried to please Him rather than myself. When I faced decisions, I quickly brought them to the feet of Jesus, seeking out His will. My life pattern needed to be lined up with God's Word.

The thought of Lordship resonated with me. My concept of being a Christian was enlarging, and my thinking was changing. I realized that how I chose to live was important. This was the beginning of a transformation. Basketball became my bridge to the truth of the gospel. For all these years, I found my security in basketball because it allowed me to be part of something bigger than myself, a safe place to belong, a place of success. This new understanding revealed that my true freedom was in the Lord Jesus Christ. Now how was I going to live this out?

My defiance toward authority seemed to change the most. I did not change completely over night, but there was a definite shift in my thinking. I found myself in less and less trouble. My identity was basketball, but after this it shifted to a whole new level. I now was told I was a new creation, a very different identity. Something was changed, and that meant my choices and actions should reflect it.

The FCA conference clarified and deepened my salvation decision. Coach Lahodny said I returned from the conference a changed person. Although I exhibited more boldness, I also displayed more self-control. I became more serious about pleasing God with my life and more sensitive to others. I kept putting myself in places to grow, and growth came in increments.

Sometimes my coach's instructions caused things to fall into place. This FCA conference did that for me spiritually. My desire to know my God more fully resulted in learning how He thinks by daily exposing myself to His Word. The more I learned, the more I could own His thinking. As I communicated with Him through prayer, I learned how to change my mind about who I was, how I fit into this world, and how to face the unknown, unafraid. This was true freedom. An additional benefit of the FCA conference was that before the conference, I never considered that college could be an option for me. I sensed my mind changing.

NATURAL BORN LEADER

Throughout my high school career Coach encouraged me to stay focused on the end goal of playing college ball. Although sports were important to both of us, she emphasized academics equally and impressed upon me the importance of a college education.

I just let her talk.

Academics meant nothing to me. Going to school was just something you had to do; grades weren't a motivation, and they didn't drive me. If I had an upcoming test, I ignored it until maybe the night before or the morning of the test. That was my only preparation. Mom only required that my siblings and I never bring home D's or F's, so this careless attitude worked fine for me.

Coach believed in me even when I didn't believe in myself. She always spoke highly of me though others criticized my lackadaisical attitude. God gave Coach eyes to see my value beyond basketball. She knew what the Word of God said:

> **"'For I know the plans I have for you,' declares the Lord, 'plans to prosper you and not to harm you, plans to give you a hope and a future.'" Jeremiah 29:11**

c. 1986. Coach Lahodny and Alexis.

She knew God's sovereignty, but I hadn't grasped it yet. My poor behavior wouldn't lead me to a hopeful future, and it needed to change. The Lord put patient, loving people in my life while I was still foolish to show me I had a hope and a future. I was just beginning to understand the bigger picture. God Himself was to be involved with my life and my decisions. He wanted to be in charge of it all.

Coach said I was a "superhero" on the court and my reputation as a basketball player was growing in South Texas. She even said, "I can see you're a natural-born leader and role model."

Shocked, I told her, "I don't want to be a leader or role model."

Coach insisted, "God put you on that path. You can't outrun your destiny!"

Her belief in me changed my life. She was like a second mom to all who were under her influence.

In fact, Marsha Sharp, the women's basketball coach at Texas Tech, said, "Jan Lahodny is the best high school coach in the whole state of Texas."

I was privileged to be under her mentoring wing.

THE BIG GAMES—SENIOR YEAR

By my senior year, our team was close, like sisters. In fact, we sang a special motivational song often and loudly. We sang it on the bus, in the locker room, wherever we were. This song was our anthem and everyone knew it. All of us had the security of being part of this team, knowing we had each other's backs.

Ten team members were seniors. Our theme was "We Shall Return," meaning we intended to return to the State Tournament, this time to win. Early in the season, we lost to a team we should have conquered. Coach played the video of that game so often it burned into our heads. We looked at our mistakes, saw places where skills were weak, and revealed our poor choices. We realized that no matter how many times we watched it, we still lost at the end. This inspired us to work harder. As a team, we matured and finally gelled into a winning team. Our season record was an amazing 33 wins and only 3 losses. We returned to the University of Texas-Austin for the State Tournament.

This time, Coach Lahodny kept our whereabouts a secret from the fans and families. Under no circumstances would her team face the final game exhausted again. Our final opponent in the championship game was Tyler Lee High School.

Huddled together as a team, hands layered together, we yelled out our motto for that year, "We shall return!"

Dropping hands, we ran onto the court, proudly wearing our matching red and white sweat suits.

We had a sense of pride because we'd made it to the Championship, and a confidence the win might be ours. We needed to deliver. Coach had taught us triple D: Determination, the willingness to go on long after the feeling has passed; Dedication, through hard work; and a Desire to finish strong by leaving it all on the court. The Victoria Stingerettes were functioning as a single entity. But we knew Tyler Lee was a worthy opponent deserving our respect.

At the end of warm-up, the team gathered at our bench for Coach's pre-game pep talk, when she reminded us of all we had accomplished to get to this game. After the singing of the National Anthem, the starting line-ups were introduced.

I heard my name called for the last time in my high school career, "Number 41, 5'6 1/2" Point Guard from Victoria, Texas, ALEXIS WARE!"

Fans cheered as I ran between my teammates lined up on both sides, giving high fives. After shaking hands with the opponent's coach, I took my spot at center court and waited for the rest of the introductions. Adrenalin flowed through my veins.

After the tip-off, the championship game began intensely. The scores bounced back and forth, back and forth. It was clear that the players on both sides wanted to win. The Stingerettes chased after every loose ball, reached for every rebound, finessed for the best shots possible, all while encouraging each other.

As the starting point guard and a leader on the court, I needed to hear the coach shout instructions for our team. The din of the whole gym made this nearly impossible. However, because I was so tuned in to Coach's voice above all, I heard her most of the time. Often, she also held up posterboard signs for me with the names of plays we had practiced all week. My role was to communicate this to the team by yelling the plays out to them.

The fans, cheerleaders, team, and coaches screamed the whole time. Their passion and encouragement drove us to play with focus. Although the team heard the ear-piercing shouting, it was only background. The only voice we heard was the coach. She knew what it would take to win a championship. We trusted her voice because she had already won two state championships.

Fear and excitement filled my mind and emotions. Fear that we might lose; excitement that we might win and be recognized as the best of the best girls' basketball team in the whole state of Texas. But the biggest bonus would be making Coach proud of us! All year long, she gave us the vision of winning this game, telling us everything we accomplished all year long had led us to this moment. Could we give her another championship?

When the buzzer sounded, the final score was Victoria 57, Tyler Lee 44. We were ecstatic, jubilant, and out-of-our-minds exhausted. We did it. Our hard work paid off. This time we didn't celebrate too soon.

We were the 1986 5A Girls' Texas State Basketball Championship Team!

Although we were winners most of time that year, Coach Lahodny and Mona Garrett from FCA were very intentional about instructing us how to win with grace and how to lose with grace. They taught the team members how to be persons of fine character on and off the court. Our reputation was as beasts on the court and ladies off the court.

After the game, we invited Tyler Lee to join us at center court for prayer. The Victoria Stingerettes were known throughout the region as the team that would pray with their opponents after each game.

Because of the deep level of respect both teams had for each other, Tyler Lee's team gathered with us in the middle of the basketball court to make a circle, alternating players holding hands to pray together. Both teams thanked God for the outcome of the game, thanking Him for no injuries, blessing each team, and reciting the Lord's Prayer.

c. 1986. Alexis holding the 5A Girls Texas State Basketball State Championship trophy.

NO PASS, NO PLAY

After basketball season, Coach reminded me I needed to take the SAT exam, so I could attend college. Actually, I didn't even know what this was, nor did I understand how important it was. I didn't prepare for it, nor did I take it seriously. I simply didn't care.

On a Saturday morning, I went to the SAT testing site, full of nerves. After reading the first few questions, I realized I didn't know these things. Anxiety filled me, and I panicked. I'd been told that if I didn't know an answer, choose "B." That's what I did. The ticking clock pressured me into filling in all the bubbles, rather than checking for right answers. I turned in the test and walked out, knowing I didn't do well, but somehow still hoping that I did.

In 1984, the Texas legislature passed a "No Pass, No Play" regulation which required students in sports to maintain a 2.0 GPA and a particular score on the SAT. The NCAA also established eligibility requirements for student athletes. I met the requirements for GPA, but when my SAT scores came back, they were in the lower 50%. I cried. Disappointed, embarrassed, and insecure, I realized my college potential was on the line. Because my identity was wrapped up with basketball and this test score could pull the plug on basketball, I stood on unstable ground.

Coach suggested I retake the exam. I didn't enjoy taking it the first time, and I sure didn't want to take it a second time. Besides, what if my scores were even lower the second time? How humiliating would that be? The fear of failing again made me refuse. I opted not to take the test again.

My past was catching up with me. All those years of cutting up, making others laugh, and barely getting by academically began to surface. Years of studying to only pass a test, rather than actually learning something, proved to be disastrous. I lost confidence in my abilities and perceived I was a failure.

Before I took the SAT test, I was being recruited by several NCAA Division One colleges. Coach took a lot of calls from colleges who wanted me to play on their teams. Now, because of my low SAT score, the calls stopped. No one was interested in providing me a basketball scholarship. Crying my eyes out in Coach's office, she suggested another option, that I attend a junior college and still play. This seemed like a slap in the face. I refused because, in my mind, I was too good a player for that. My pride wouldn't let me consider it.

Winning was my true motivation on the court. When I lost all those opportunities to play college basketball, it felt just like losing an important game. My pride and refusal to retake the SAT stood in the way of playing college ball. This was a huge blow. My future was disappearing before my eyes. I had thought my basketball skills would carry me anywhere I wanted, but now the door slammed shut.

The weeks that followed brought me to a new place of humility. Basketball was my life. My eyes couldn't see beyond high school. As I walked the halls of Victoria High, my reputation as a skilled basketball player took second place to the new reputation of failure. I became paranoid, thinking everyone knew I failed the test and wouldn't be playing college basketball. The last two months of my senior year were spent in the shameful disappointment that I'd let down Coach, my school, and my family.

Instead of taking the next step toward college, I had messed it all up. Everything I believed about myself evaporated into thin air along with my pride. These were difficult days of uncertainty and hopelessness. My pride and arrogance were totally crushed. I cried more tears than I've ever cried.

What would I do now? Who was I anyway? Now what?

I was unraveling.

CHAPTER 2

TEXAS TECH

FACE TO FACE

If you want to play college basketball, I'll do my best to get you a scholarship somewhere."

Coach's words echoed in my ears. She had invited me to her house to have lunch with Marsha Sharp, women's basketball coach at Texas Tech University. Because Coach Lahodny had a two-year-old son, Buck, an informal meal at her house was easier. Her country home was a place of comfort since I had been there before. This would be a meeting like no other; however, I was oblivious to its importance. Coach always had my back, so I trusted her choices for me.

When I arrived, the two coaches stood together outside, and I sensed that they'd been talking about me. Insecurity engulfed me again because I started to realized how critical this meeting would be to me.

Coach welcomed me and said, "Alexis, I want you to meet Marsha Sharp."

I boldly put my hand out to shake hers, hoping she wouldn't sense my turmoil.

She extended her hand and said kindly, "Hi, Alexis."

I said, "Nice to meet you."

Together, we walked inside to the living room. Buck was playing on the floor, and his presence helped ease the tension. We sat on the floor, playing mini-basketball with him. I knew that Coach Sharp had seen videos of my games and practices, and that she saw talent in me. Also, I knew she'd heard of my reputation as a talented basketball player in the schools in south Texas. However, there was still the matter of my terrible SAT score. Yet she was still willing to consider me for her team. It stunned me when I realized a Division One college might still be a viable option. I knew I didn't deserve it. Usually, I received negative consequences when I messed up, but this felt like something good was about to happen.

She offered me a full scholarship! That meant my college tuition, room-and-board, and books would be fully covered. Unfortunately, because of my low SAT score, I couldn't play basketball my freshman year; instead, I needed to concentrate on academics. At that moment, the lack of basketball wasn't as important as the fact that I was invited to join the Texas Tech team. This invitation gave me a sense of importance, an assurance that I wouldn't be humiliated by that low score. I could go to college and redeem myself. It was a second chance to do academics right.

The three of us talked through the pros: I would go to college at Texas Tech and eventually play for them. Coach Sharp made it clear that she wanted me on her team and wanted to take this chance on me. We discussed the cons: No basketball for a whole year.

As the visit progressed, Coach Sharp must have seen how much love and respect Coach Lahodny had for me. And my passion to be part of the Texas Tech program spilled into my voice. Both coaches assured me that they had faith I could succeed in my academics. Because they believed, I began to believe it, too.

By the end of that meeting, I agreed to all the terms and limitations of accepting the scholarship from Texas Tech, including waiting to play for one year. Walking away, I was on Cloud 9. I hoped that my future would again include basketball. The encouraging words the coaches spoke into my life took root. The initial apprehension had melted away. Driving away I felt validated, valued, and victorious.

Although I wanted to play my freshman year, Coach Sharp said, "Sometimes God opens windows instead of doors, and you just have to climb out of them!"

This was my only window of opportunity, and it was only slightly open. Still, it was a glimmer of hope. Of course I gratefully accepted, determined to turn a corner and walk toward a new future. Although my acceptance was humble, grateful and understated, inside my heart was soaring. Surely, Coach Sharp heard the gratitude in my voice.

On the other side of this window was my beloved basketball again. One day I'd be running up and down the Texas Tech basketball courts, shooting baskets. Coach Sharp and Texas Tech were taking a huge risk with me.

Texas Tech, located in Lubbock, Texas, was 500 miles away from Victoria. In the fall of 1986, all alone and inexperienced, I got on a bus with total strangers, to ride the eighteen hours to Lubbock. It took so long because there were lots of stops. I'd never ridden a bus like this before, so every stop alarmed me, wondering if it was my stop. The driver assured me he'd let me know. This was one of the scariest things I'd ever done. I was so very alone.

For the first time, I left my family behind. Sadness overwhelmed me. As the bus moved away from the station, tears welled up, and lonliness overwhelmed me. All the support and love my family gave me was in the back window, growing smaller.

When I arrived in Lubbock, the assistant coach met me at the bus station and loaded up all my boxes. She took me to the dorm and helped me unload, before leaving me with strangers. My roommate wasn't there yet, so I was alone, wondering what was next.

Because of my athletic scholarship, I was housed with the other athletes, but I had no practices, no uniform, no games, and no glory. Finally, reality was sinking in. No one knew me, I knew no one either. With my athletic identity stripped, I fit nowhere. My identity was gone, and I didn't know who Alexis Ware was anymore. I was a believer in Christ, but my identity had been Christ and basketball. Now all that had changed.

During this season without basketball, I found that the world was Christ and me alone. This difficult experience of feeling almost nonexistent for months taught me a valuable lesson, so I learned to apply myself academically, and I also learned the value of listening to someone who cared for me. I embraced that my identity was in Christ and nothing more.

"Whoever gives heed to instruction prospers, and blessed is the one who trusts in the Lord." Proverbs 16:20

Finally, my faith was choosing to trust and submit to God's instructions because He had my ultimate good at heart, and ahead of me were blessings.

ALL BOOKS; NO BASKETBALL

"My name is Alexis Ware," I told my roommate. I waited for her to be impressed.

She just looked at me and said, "My name is Reena Lynch."

Shocked, I said, "Don't you know who I am?"

"No!" she replied. "Don't you know who I am?"

"You mean you've never heard of Alexis Ware?" I said in disbelief.

"No. You mean you've never heard of Reena Lynch?"

c. 1990. Alexis and her college roommate, Reena Lynch.

We were both basketball stars, but from different parts of Texas. I was well known in South Texas, but she was equally well known in West Texas. We were full of ourselves. Turns out we "superstars" were unknowns in other parts of Texas. Nobody in South Texas had ever heard of the "superior" skills of Reena Lynch. Nobody in West Texas had ever heard of the "fabulous" Alexis Ware.

Even though Reena and I had a rocky start, we became best friends. During that freshman year, she played in all the games. I only watched. Because I couldn't play, I attended all the home games as a fan. This gave me the opportunity to see the dynamic between the coach and the team. Occasionally, if Coach was hard on them, I'd tell them they'd make up for it in the next game. Sometimes, I encouraged them to not take things so personally. Reena said she sensed the support I gave the team was invaluable. I saw how rough it was for her to transition from high school to college ball. The team knew they could count on encouragement from me. I became the team's off-court cheerleader.

Because I lived with the athletes, good people with goals and skills surrounded me. However, when a teammate broke curfew, the whole team had to run the football stadium at 6 a.m. for punishment. That meant everyone ran the steps from the top to the bottom, all around the stadium. This was brutal. The extreme punishment encouraged the team to handle their own infractions, preventing issues from ever reaching the coaches. They were learning to police themselves and hold themselves accountable to each other. I was so glad I didn't have to run the stadium during that first year.

VALUABLE FRIENDSHIP

The Christian disciplines I began in the 10th grade through FCA were still my daily practice. Reena remembers that I rose at 7:00 a.m. every morning, got out my Bible, read, and cranked up Christian music.

One day, after playing an away game and getting in very late, Reena was awakened from an exhausted sleep by my loud Christian music.

She yelled, "HEY!" and folded her pillow around her head.

I quickly turned the music down for her.

Reena always treated me with respect and valued my relationship with God. Often, we'd crank up old gospel songs on my cassette player and sing into our hairbrushes.

My freshman year, I wanted to succeed not just athletically (eventually), but academically. All freshmen athletes were required to attend a daily study hall. There, I learned some new and helpful study skills. Never again in my college career did academics keep me from achieving my goals. God was teaching me to value godly counsel and to work "as unto the Lord." Academics were no longer a problem but had become a goal. God's work ethic was taking root.

My motto had become, "Don't stop. Don't quit. Keep going."

But to do that, I needed to give it my all, no matter what.

As my coach always said, "Leave everything on the court."

Even if that court is a classroom.

FREEDOM?

The college environment brought out a different kind of socializing for me. I realized there was new freedom. There were no boundaries. Wow! No one told us when to go to bed, or to clean our rooms, or to study, or to wash our clothes. Such freedom!

Because I was at Texas Tech on an athletic scholarship, I was thrown into the mix with all the athletes. One Friday night two handsome football players paid attention to me. They were strong, athletic, fun, and so fine; the whole package. Since I was friendly (and naïve), I invited both up to my room. We had such a great time laughing, talking, and just having fun. One thing led to another. I didn't catch on as they exchanged glances, trying to decide who would leave, and who would stay. Eventually one guy departed, leaving me with the other. Soon, the guy and I were hugging, rubbing, kissing, bumping and grinding. No alcohol or drugs were involved. I was sober, aware and completely clothed, but walking on dangerously thin ice. We were getting lost in the moment when suddenly, the phone rang. It triggered an alarm that went off in my mind.

I jumped to answer the phone and thought, "What am I doing?"

Long before, when I entered Crain Middle School in Victoria, Texas, I knew some girls got a lot of attention being sexually inappropriate with boys. At that age, the girls were noticing the boys noticing us. I overheard conversations about sex. When the gossip spoke of girls who were sexually active already, the conversation was tinged with shame and condemnation. I determined not to be one of those girls. This sex-outside-of-marriage thing wasn't for me. I quietly, but firmly committed to not have sex until I was married.

But here I was in college testing that commitment.

When I got off the phone, I turned back to the guy and told him he needed to leave. Of course, he tried to persuade me otherwise.

I told him, "No, no. You've got to go! You've got to go now!"

He finally left.

The freedom of a college life had turned the tables on me. The world told me I was free to have sex outside of marriage... no one was going to stop me. However, I saw that freedom could quickly become a trap if I didn't rein it in.

Sitting on my bed, my heart pounded and these thoughts ran through my head:

- I'm on a full basketball scholarship. I've nearly put myself in a position of losing it all.
- I might have also put myself at risk for contracting an STD or becoming pregnant.
- I might have taken the chance of developing a bad reputation.
- I came close to failing myself by not maintaining my personal standards and disappointing my family, my teammates and coaches who depended on me.
- I would disappoint my Savior who died for me.

> **"Do you not know that your bodies are temples of the Holy Spirit, Who is in you, Whom you have received from God? You are not your own; you were bought at a price. Therefore honor God with your bodies." I Corinthians 6:19-20**

After this incident, I realized that even though I had standards, I needed a set of boundaries to protect those standards. Boundaries define. They are limits we use to protect ourselves and others. I needed to set boundaries before entering any relationship. I needed to make decisions with a cool head, rather than in the heat of the moment.

My boundary was no sex of any kind until marriage. Just like in any sport, when the referee blows the whistle, the play should stop. But if the players continue after that, there's great confusion for the players, coaches and fans. That isn't how the game should be played. When rules are broken, the result is chaos.

My referee was Jesus Christ, and He set my boundaries. I decided that if someone questioned my boundaries or pressured me to abandon them, I need to "hear the whistle." That's when the "play" stopped. If I continued to play after the "whistle has been blown," the game was no longer fun or fair.

Just because there was a lot of sexual activity around me, I didn't have to participate. My boundaries were set when I had a level head. My freedom came from embracing the values of God's Word.

> **"...do not share in the sins of others. Keep yourself pure."**
> **1 Timothy 5:22b**

I set a new boundary of no more hugging, rubbing, kissing, bumping or grinding. Why? Because I want to remain a virgin till married, but also my heart's desire was to be pure in all things. That meant I wanted to please the Lord above all, more than pleasing a man or even myself. If I became physically involved with a man without the intention of having sex, I'd be unfair and misleading. Physical touch has a natural progression which is designed to lead to sexual intercourse. Instead, I believe sex is a beautiful thing designed to enhance and empower the relationship between a husband and wife.

Another new boundary was that I wouldn't invite any man into my home without other people being there. Why? Because I didn't want to put myself or him at risk. Maintaining this boundary kept things from happening right up front. These self-imposed boundaries allowed me to guard my heart.

"Above all else, guard your heart, for everything you do flows from it." Proverbs 4:23

REAL FREEDOM

Sometimes I did feel left out because I wasn't doing what everyone else was doing. Although I dated a little, I noticed that most relationships diminished after three months. I'd refuse to have sex, so they broke up with me. I often faced a battle of rejection that left me feeling unwanted. I realized my feelings and the truth could be two different things. Also, feelings don't dictate truth. Deep within, I knew the truth, and I still believed I was someone of value and worth.

Oftentimes people told me, "You might miss out on something."

I knew part of that "something" could be STD's, unplanned pregnancy, a broken heart and a fragmented self to present to my future husband. Who would mind missing out on those things?

"Something must be wrong with you."

"You're missing out."

"I can't believe you haven't had sex already."

"Have you never had a boyfriend?"

"Are you scared?"

These are a few of the comments I heard about my personal choice to not have sex before marriage. The decision I made in junior high and reconfirmed as a college freshman never wavered. Despite peer pressure, hormones and f-i-n-e looking guys, I chose not to have sex while I was in college. I made it through without giving myself away.

"I hold fast to your statutes, Lord; do not let me be put to shame." Psalms 119:31

Because I chose not to have sex in college, it freed me to have a wealth of healthy relationships. No guilt. No shame. No consequences. On graduation day I walked across the stage with something more than a degree in my hand. I also carried my virginity and a clear conscience.

A NEW MINDSET

Overall, putting off athletics during my freshman year allowed me to grow up. Putting on the new me, meant that I had to make choices, God-pleasing choices. Pride hadn't served me well, in fact it brought me to destruction. That had to be replaced with humility. During most of my college years, I participated in several on-campus Christian organizations, such as Campus Crusade for Christ, The Wesley Foundation and Fellowship of Christian Athletes. Attending all their weekly meetings and occasional retreats kept me focused on the Lord, growing in Him, and joining with other believers. Through the scriptural teaching I understood how Jesus could truly be my Lord.

> **"You were taught, with regard to your former way of life, to put off your old self, which is being corrupted by its deceitful desires; to be made new in the attitude of your minds; and to put on the new self, created to be like God in true righteousness and holiness." Ephesians 4:22-24**

Realizing my identity was in Christ set my priorities in a different order. Assigning more importance to academics, I never missed a class. I encouraged my teammates and learned how to live with a roommate. But through it all, I missed basketball. I needed to get back on the court.

c. 1987. Playing for Athletes in Action.

c. 1986. Alexis played #20 on
the AIA Summer Team.

CHAPTER 3

ATHLETES IN ACTION

BASKETBALL AGAIN

Anxiety filled my mind as I boarded the biggest airplane I'd ever seen for my first international flight. I was trapped on a jet flying sixteen hours from America to Brazil. Oddly, as we ascended, the air pressure didn't equalize in my head; instead, it increased, and I could do nothing. I needed to get off and go home, but that wasn't possible. I was helpless. My head was splitting, as fear washed over me. I couldn't help it, I cried. All that fear had to go somewhere, so it ran down my face. To balance the increasing pressure in my ear, my friends handed me chewing gum. I chewed several pieces, but the pressure didn't release. Nothing worked until we landed hours later.

How did I end up in Brazil? God led me there, and I obeyed Him.

Following my freshman year in 1987, Coach Sharp suggested that I apply to play for Athletes-In-Action (AIA), a branch of Campus Crusade for Christ. She encouraged me to think about traveling with their Christian women's basketball team. AIA tours all over the world in the summers, playing other women's teams and sharing personal testimonies of faith. Just as He'd used my high school coach, the Lord was using my college coach to set me up for a "win." After sitting out my freshman year, I wanted to rejoin the excitement of basketball, so I enthusiastically accepted the AIA invitation.

To participate in AIA, I needed to raise funds to pay for my expenses. Coach Sharp encouraged me to send out letters for sponsorship. Money came in quickly. The request was even published in the Victoria Advocate, my hometown newspaper, and many people responded. I was shocked to get a donation from Miss Avery, the music teacher from Roland Elementary School in Victoria, Texas. During elementary school, I frequented the principal's office so often that eventually they passed me on to the music teacher. Miss Avery became my favorite teacher. A gentle, kind-spirited person, she had a way with words and mannerisms that were calming and inviting to me. When she talked with me about my behavior, I listened. I didn't want to disappoint her, but just being in her room meant I had done something wrong. Somehow I always left feeling better and believing I wasn't a disappointment. Although she was living in Europe serving as a missionary, Miss Avery still sent support to encourage me. I was so surprised that she remembered me. Miss Avery said she was proud of me and the work I was getting ready to do. Other than my family, she was the first person I felt truly believed in me and my potential. And she was still showing me that support all these years later. That made me feel loved and valuable.

AIA BRAZIL AND PERU

Before leaving on summer tour in 1987, the AIA gathered the women athletes for a month of training. We needed to pray and study together to form a cohesive team. We were going to Brazil and Peru, which was my first time out of the country. I was apprehensive. No. Actually, I was terrified.

After that traumatic plane ride, we landed and boarded a bus at the airport. It was dark. I sat at the back, right in front of the luggage and kept hearing crying noises coming from the baggage. Scared, I told the driver about the noises. When he investigated, he found a dirty, scrawny little boy hanging on the open back window, moaning. The bus driver shooed him away, and he ran into the darkness. When we asked our translators about it, he said many children were starving, and they often choose the airport to ask people for food. We were shocked and saddened that we hadn't given him food. That was my first experience with poverty in another country.

BRAZILIAN EXPERIENCES

Our AIA team, dressed alike in our blue and white sweat jackets and pants, were taken to a shopping mall. We split into several small groups. Eventually, some of our members were escorted by security to the mall office, and they didn't know why. For some reason, the translator wasn't around, so they were helpless. My small group passed by the window and were shocked to see our teammates inside. We could tell they had been detained. Fear gripped our hearts for just a moment. We frantically searched for our translator, found him and he straightened things out. Their "crime" was that they were all dressed alike, causing a big distraction. When they were released, we all had a good laugh.

Traveling across Brazil, we saw and experienced new things. Because I was such a newcomer to travel, many things caught me off guard. Friends were insistent, so in Rio de Janeiro, I traveled up Corcovado Mountain in a local taxi to see one of the new Seven Wonders of the World. The driver, obviously familiar with this road, drove much too fast and much too close to the edge. The narrow road barely accommodated two cars passing.

Looking out the window, there was nothing but space between our cab and the ground far, far below. I thought we might die.

We made it successfully to the top and saw the famous huge white statue of "Christ, the Redeemer." This 125-foot tall work of art, created by several artists from different places in the world, was breathtaking. Because of my relationship with Christ, this figure took on a greater meaning. I loved that this display pointed the world to my Christ. It pleased me to see how this Christ-statue was visible for miles, drawing everyone who saw it to thoughts of Jesus.

Peace rested on this mountain top. I embraced that peace and reflected on God's goodness. The 92-foot arm stretch reminded me that Christ is available to all people in all the world. His arms are open wide.

The scary taxi ride to the top reminded me that in this world of turmoil, we still move toward the mountain top. There, the end of the journey, is where we find Jesus and everlasting peace.

99 POINTS BEHIND

For one basketball game, we played the Brazilian National Team, the top players they sent to the Olympics. We were outclassed, like a middle school team trying to play against a college team. The gym had no air conditioning, and it was a hot Brazilian summer day. Every teammate was drenched with sweat. We were encouraged to drink a lot to stay hydrated, but because we couldn't drink the water in Brazil, we were given Cokes—hot canned cokes. Nobody complained because we needed something to drink. The burst of sugar created a sugar high, then a sugar crash. But still we needed to keep drinking and playing.

Right before the game ended, one of our women attempted and made a half-court shot. We cheered so loudly that the audience was fascinated. True, we lost the game by 99 points, but we were so pumped by the success of that final shot. Our celebration for those few points caused people to stick around for our message. They listened attentively to our testimonies, and many responded through a questionnaire that would be followed up with by local Christian churches.

We played basketball games with local teams in the evenings, but throughout the day we took part in other missions. During our week in Sao Paulo, the AIA teams (men and women) hosted a daily Christian Camp for children. The camp was held outside on packed dirt. We formed small teams, and taught them shooting, dribbling, and passing drills, and then we played games against each other. My team was called the Lakers, and we wore yellow mesh vests.

All week, I led the group in an old song, "I Want to Be More like Jesus." In fact, because we sang it so often, everyone said it was my song. On the final day, suddenly, the children sang to us in Portuguese. Music was a common language. When they finished singing, my teammates encouraged me to sing my song again.

I want to be more
And more like Jesus
Everyday!

Because it's a catchy song, and they heard it every day, everyone picked it up quickly. The whole amphitheater joined in and we all sang in unison—the AIA teams, the children, the staff. As the music swelled, tears flowed.

Marcia, a withdrawn little Brazilian girl was on my camp team. I'm always drawn to those who are isolated and insecure, so I grabbed a translator to seek her out. I encouraged her to just stay by my side. She stayed close the whole week, so we developed a relationship, though we couldn't speak the same language. The last day, as we were saying good-byes, Marcia ran away from the group, crying. I noticed and followed. When I reached her, I gave her a hug.

She clung tightly and whispered in Portuguese, "I will see you in heaven!"

I cried, too. I'd spent the week with her on my team, but we had little communication, so I didn't know any details about her life. Somehow the Lord had spoken to her, and He has no language barrier.

Later I wanted to write a letter of encouragement to her, and a friend helped me pen it in her Portuguese. The truth of the gospel overrides any circumstance. Although I had no other contact with her, I know she touched my life and made me even more determined to live for the only One who holds hope.

God was giving me a greater passion for hurting people through the worship, fellowship and prayer. I saw how big God is and that His truth is the same all over the world. The mission of Christ came clear:

> **"Therefore go and make disciples of all nations, baptizing them in the name of the Father, and the Son and of Holy Spirit." Matthew 28:19**

CHAPTER 4

LET THE GAMES BEGIN

NOTHING'S THE SAME

I called Coach Lahodny crying. "I don't think I can do this. Nothing is the same. This is nothing like high school."

In 1987, my sophomore year, I was finally allowed to play on the Texas Tech team. It was overwhelming to balance academics and basketball practices. I had assumed my next coach would not only be my coach, but also my mentor, friend and guide. I was off balance with this new coach, unsure how to please her.

When I called Coach Lahodny crying, she assured me that I couldn't compare high school and college. She reminded me that coaches were different. Not every one was running things the same. Competition was more intense and I needed to learn my new teammates. Coach gave me a different perspective and reminded me that college ball was more advanced, but encouraged me that I could make the necessary changes. I returned to practice with a different motivation and a new understanding of what the college coaches expected.

Finally, I was handed all my basketball gear. I proudly accepted the red, white and black uniform and shoes, representing Texas Tech. Relief flooded my heart because I was getting my second chance. This was the year I'd get on the court and play, and I was so excited.

My teammates had already learned to play under Coach Sharp during their freshman year when all I was required to do was study. Now I needed to learn her style of basketball. As practices progressed, I found my place on the team, and the anxiety decreased. My first game was against Louisiana Tech, and I scored 24 points, surprising even myself. I was proving to Texas Tech that they were right to take a chance on me. The coaches had heard about me, but now they could see with their own eyes.

When that game ended, someone on my team said to me flippantly, "Don't get the big head."

That casual comment took root in my heart. After that, I backed away from taking so many shots. I didn't want to be known as a "ball hog." I became hesitant and fearful, second-guessing my shots. Every time I was clear to shoot the ball, I heard those words. However, when recognition came my way, I received it humbly, realizing the talent I was given came from God, and it was given for a reason, not so I could respond with personal pride.

As the semester moved on, the team became stronger and stronger. We were growing into a solid winning phenomenon. We finished third in the Southwest conference. Finishing my first year on the basketball court gave me a sense of satisfaction.

AIA-CZECHOSLOVAKIA AND RUSSIA

We were late—very late! Our AIA sponsor in Czechoslovakia had arranged for us to attend a local church service. The service had already started, and we were embarrassed. However, when the Czechs saw the AIA basketball team enter, they rose and relinquished their seats to us. In this Czech church, we were treated with respect and honor. We filed in and took those offered seats gratefully, knowing they would have to stand somewhere else. The church was overflowing with people standing at the back and others standing outside near a window. I was surprised at what they were willing to endure to hear God's Word.

As usual, we wore our sweat suits, and there was no air-conditioning. That summer of 1988 was hot. Really hot. I ripped out a sheet from my journal to fan myself. Looking around, I was the only one fanning. The Czech people were so intent on the service they didn't notice the heat. What a contrast! In America, we would have insisted on an air-conditioned building.

The service was in their language, so we needed a translator. Peter, our clean-cut Czech interpreter, had served AIA several years before and was a professed atheist. He had a negative attitude working for a paycheck and nothing more. However, he had to interpret our words as we spoke the gospel, as well as other practical things. Occasionally, he translated as someone was led to the Lord. The AIA players were kind and respectful to him. Players who'd known him before were astounded when, at his request, he translated for AIA again. This time, they said, his attitude was different, changed. He was genuinely engaged in interpreting. Several times each day, he interpreted the gospel message which confronted him with the words his mouth was saying. Several times each day, he watched the AIA teams love the Czech people with a genuine concern for their souls.

Because Peter translated the sermon, we listened closely. The sermon and our doctrinal beliefs aligned in many ways, which meant we were all serving the same God.

After the service, people swamped us. An older gentleman with a mustache grabbed my face with his warm hands, kissed me on my forehead, and shouted, "Africa!"

Shocked, I answered him with a big grin, "No, America!"

Everybody laughed.

The basketball team was tall and obviously foreign, so everyone stared. We smiled and waved. My smile attracts children. It also helped that I was American. When I began to pass out the AIA brochures, containing our pictures, our mission, and the gospel message, I drew a crowd.

The brochure's gospel message was simply stated so that the children could understand it. Without my knowing, an elderly, fragile gray-haired lady stood off to the side listening intently. When she came over, I asked Peter to translate. Through Peter, she gently asked questions as we led her through the brochure. The brochure's final page invited her to give her life to Christ.

I asked her, "Does this sound like something you want to do?"

Confidently, she said, "I want to do that!"

I led her through a prayer acknowledging her desire to belong to Christ, Peter translating, and she responding through him. She was the first person the Lord had ever allowed me to lead into relationship with Him. I was amazed to the core that God would use an American basketball player to interrupt this lady's life with the gospel. To God be the glory.

Because of who we were, how we carried ourselves, and how we loved them, the people were more willing to hear what the AIA basketball team had to say about Jesus.

ATTITUDE CHECK

AIA fed my passion for sharing the gospel, but it also challenged me to leave behind my childish ways. Temple Elmore, my AIA roommate, had played for the College of Charleston. She was a former All-American post player, yet spoke with a gentle manner—when she spoke at all. When Temple talked, people listened because her words carried wisdom and authority. As roommates, she began to speak constructively to me. During travel in Czechoslovakia, I often went to extremes to get a laugh from the team. If something got too serious, I needed to lighten the mood with a funny remark. Serious emotions made me uncomfortable, and I used humor against it.

Temple often said, "You play too much! Get it together."

How could she criticize me, I wondered, when we didn't know each other? Her words hurt, but I had to admit they were true words.

Finally, one day Temple said, "Nobody's going to take you seriously! You are always so silly, trying to get attention. You make everything a joke."

This was a wake-up call because I didn't realize how obnoxious I'd become. I needed to change. I worked to pare back my unruly actions, and to balance humor with leadership. When the four-week tour ended, and we sat in a debrief session, she stood to share with everyone.

She leveled her eyes firmly on me and said with authority, "You passed the test!"

"What test?"

"I wanted to help you understand that you're a leader, but if you couldn't take things seriously, no one would take you seriously."

Temple, had become a big sister to me because she was willing to speak truth.

"As iron sharpens iron, so one person sharpens another." Proverbs 27:17

AIA-MOSCOW, RUSSIA

"No, you stupid American!" shouted the angry woman on the street of Moscow.

We'd secretly offered her one of our team's brochures. We walked away giggling, amused that she knew that much English.

After our two-week tour in Czechoslovakia, we took our games to Moscow. In those Cold War days, Christianity was forbidden in Russia. However, AIA could travel there because we were a sports team. We could share the gospel only at halftime, no outside mission efforts in the streets.

The Cold War stereotypes took over my perceptions. I wanted to like the people, but they seemed unapproachable, and I didn't feel welcome. I became fascinated by the colorful onion domes on the buildings. The breathtaking beauty of that architecture eclipsed everything else. During our week in Moscow, we were housed in a hotel. The people we interacted with were Russian staffers from the Campus Crusade organization in Moscow. Because we were a Christian group, fans from other Christian churches followed us. My preconceived ideas about Russians began to crumble as we became acquainted with our fans. Over the course of our time there, we had many conversations and sensed a connection by the end of our time.

Oddly enough, on game days the opposing teams often rode with us to the gym where we would be playing. This gave us a golden opportunity to share the gospel with the basketball players since our brochures were printed in Russian.

In the early 1990's, McDonald's opened their first store in Moscow. The familiar golden arches were proudly displayed on a large gray wall and on the front of the first floor of a larger building. The restaurant was so popular. Because it was one of a few fast-food restaurants, people waited in huge lines. When the AIA team went, we stood out, and were treated like royalty. Standing in line for hours, we needed a diversion. We sang the same simple gospel song we sang in Brazil. Those around us loved it, smiling and gesturing. It was nonverbal communication, but we still knew we were accepted. It was a real McMoment.

During our trip to Czechoslovakia and Russia, we practiced an interesting AIA custom. We traded our game gear and gospel tracts with our opposing team: t-shirts, shoes, warm-ups, socks, shirts, shorts, etc. This gave everyone— American, Czech, and Russian—a souvenir. Selfishly, I never gave up my shoes. But I came back to Texas Tech in the fall of 1988 with several t-shirts, lots of memories, and a deeper walk with God.

c. 1990. Alexis, #32, in action as a Texas Tech Lady Raider.

CHAPTER 5

A SEASON OF INJURY

HURT AND HEARTACHE

I stole the ball and drove in for the shot. Looking back while in the air, I twisted my whole body to locate the Louisiana Tech player because it's a shameful thing to get your shot blocked. For a split second, I took my eyes off the goal and went down hard. My knee buckled and sent shock waves throughout my entire body. The crowd made a corporate gasp and the gym fell silent.

I was hurt, and I knew it.

It was only the second game of my junior season. When I crumpled to the floor gripping my knee, I knew I would not be able to get up because of the blinding pain. Our trainer trotted to my side and demanded I stand up.

I couldn't.

Several teammates came out, lifted me up, and I hobbled off the floor. The trainer and I went to the locker room because she needed a better look at my knee. Meanwhile, I was lost in the pain, crying. She put an ice bag on my knee to bring down the rapid swelling. Already, I couldn't straighten out my leg. She gave me crutches and told me to ice the knee at regular intervals, assuming I'd be fine.

Thoughts bombarded my mind all night long. Coach Sharp had given me so many opportunities, first academic, now athletic. I was devastated because I perceived that I was disappointing her and the team. As the long, sleepless night went on, my emotional agony overrode the physical pain. After a pain-filled night, I returned to Lubbock with the team.

At the next practice, still on crutches and still in pain, I told the trainer I needed to see a doctor. She assumed I was just scared about the injury and being a big baby. She thought, or so it seemed, that I was faking an injury, which made no sense. Why would I want to sit out another year? Did others think I was faking too? At the humiliating thought, my old insecurities took over my thinking. After talking directly to Coach Sharp, the trainer was ordered to take me to the doctor.

Fortunately, the X-rays showed no broken bones, so I thought I was off the hook.

But the doctor said, "You have blown everything out in your knee."

"What does that mean?" I asked.

"It means you won't be playing for the rest of the school year."

I needed total reconstructive surgery. I burst into tears.

My anger became directed toward the trainer, and I told her, "Don't touch me!"

The shock of this diagnosis and prognosis put me in a dark place. I was so furious, so heartbroken that my basketball career was on hold. Again.

Later, I went to the hospital in Lubbock where doctors did major reconstructive surgery to repair my ligaments, cartilage, and kneecap. When I awoke from surgery, I wore a cast from my hip to my ankle, molded at such an angle that my leg was slightly bent. And that's where it stayed for three weeks.

Because the cast held my leg stationary, scar tissue built up in my knee. After the cast was removed, the trainer had to take over my rehab. Every time we met, five days a week, she tried to tear up that tissue. She pushed down on my knee, trying to extend it. I screamed in alarm and pain, crying, which was embarrassing because I was in the rehab room with other injured men and women athletes. Healing came so slowly, I began to wonder if this had taken me out of basketball for good. But the therapy continued because my knee had to be released from the bent position. For six months, this painful pushing to straighten my knee was part of my physical therapy treatment. When I was released at the end of the Spring semester to go home, I was given exercises to strengthen my knee.

Instead of traveling and playing with the AIA program, I spent the summer of 1989 at home in Victoria, TX, rehabbing myself, wearing a protective knee brace. I still needed to practice dribbling and shooting and the brace allowed me to do that with security.

KNEE RESTORED; MIND RETRAINED

When I returned to Texas Tech in the fall of 1989, the doctor released me to play basketball, so I joyfully took to the court. My knee had healed, but my mind hadn't. With determination, I pushed through the fear and improved physically and mentally.

I played basketball again, and things were looking up. My Texas Tech uniform now included a strong knee brace to protect me from further injury and support my knee. However, it was a constant reminder of the weakness of that leg. My trainer told Coach I was protecting that leg and not playing to full capacity. My battle now, she said, was mental. My knee was good to go, but in my mind, the minute I landed on that leg, I was expecting my knee to blow out again. Because Coach saw that, she didn't play me as often.

Although I worked hard, I didn't get as much playing time, so I lost interest. I was no longer the starting point guard and sitting on the bench sapped my enthusiasm for the game. Discouragement replaced my passion.

In the middle of that season, during a game with Baylor University, I rolled my ankle on my strong leg and fell.

I was destroyed!

Beating that floor, I asked, "Why, God! Why?"

I'm not sure what hurt worse, the physical pain or the deep disappointment that I might be benched again.

It seemed I was about to enter another dark season. I imagined more months of surgery, painful rehab and loss of basketball. Although I had solidly found an identity in Christ during my freshman year, this injury taught me I still had more to learn.

It was time to confront what was true and what was a lie.

Lie: My identity was shaken.

Lie: Everything was slipping away from me.

Lie: I had no value, no usefulness.

Lie: The only thing I'm good at is playing basketball.

Instead, I needed to remember God's truth.

Truth: My security is in Christ alone.

Truth: God is in control.

Truth: My value is found in Christ.

Truth: Although I was gifted in playing basketball, I was gifted in other areas, too. My grades showed I was a good student. My teammates' willingness to follow my lead on the court revealed I was a leader. Personal relationships built on Jesus Christ exhibited my place in God's kingdom.

Those dark thoughts were lies, which couldn't stand in the light of what was true. I didn't stay in that dark place for long.

"Then you will know the truth, and the truth will set you free." John 8:32

Surprisingly, the ankle injury only took me out for one week, so I only missed one game. Still the fear of a new injury limited my performance at the highest level. I constantly reminded myself to literally walk in the truth. And the truth was, my legs were strong enough to play all-out basketball.

Through all the negative experiences and injuries, I learned lessons for life, so those experiences had value. That year caused me to place my confidence in Christ more and more.

> **"And we know that in all things God works for the good of those who love Him, who have been called according to His purpose." Romans 8:28**

Toward the end of that year, I grew weary of the responsibility of being a collegiate athlete. The full schedules, the practices, the games, the politics, the very dynamic of the team wore on me mentally, emotionally, as well as physically. At this point, I wasn't playing as much, my love of the game had faded, and I was just tired of it all. Although I had never quit anything in my life, I was ready to quit basketball.

There were a few more classes I needed to take in order to graduate. My basketball scholarship guaranteed that if I needed a fifth year to graduate, it would be covered. I sat out my freshman year due to my SAT score, and I missed most of my junior year because of my knee injury, so I was still eligible to play basketball for one more year. But I wanted to quit.

First, though, I needed to be sure the scholarship was still valid. I went to talk with Robert W. Lawless, President of Texas Tech.

"Will Texas Tech pay for my fifth year of college?" I asked him.

"Absolutely!" he said, "We promised you that."

"Great," I said. "I don't want to play basketball anymore." Walking away from his office, I knew peace. I could still finish my degree. Later that day, my phone rang; it was Coach Sharp. The president had called her. My heart pounded, wondering what she'd say and how I should respond.

"Lex, what's this I hear about you wanting to quit basketball?" Coach asked. "Can we sit down and talk about this?"

Because I respected her, I agreed.

As a Christ-follower, I wanted to be honoring to the Lord, to Texas Tech, to the coaches and my teammates. I wanted to be known as a woman of integrity, no matter what challenges I was facing.

I entered her office and sat down, filled with uncertainty.

In answer to her question, I replied, "I thought you were going to kick me off the team."

Our conversation revealed that she and I had both believed rumors we had heard about each other, rather than speaking directly to each other. We laid on the table issues of misunderstanding on both sides. During this conversation, we each spoke truth and replaced the lies. The air was finally cleared between us. Because we were both believers in Christ, we knew we must honor God in this situation.

We each finally asked, "What do you need from me?"

Coach and I had a new understanding of each other's expectations. I walked out feeling like I was free from the insecurity of not knowing where I stood. Free from playing out of fear of doing something wrong. I was now free to play without limitation.

Coach encouraged me to not give up on the one thing I really loved: basketball. I now believed she and I could be on the same page, so I stayed to play a fifth year.

LIFE OUTSIDE OF BASKETBALL

One day, my friends at Campus Crusade found out I was on the basketball team. "Why didn't you tell us you played? We would've supported you all along!"

Many times in high school, my perception was that people wanted to be my friend only because I played basketball, rather than wanting to know me personally. I felt used. This flawed and insecure thinking followed me into college.

"Because I didn't want people to connect to me just because I am a basketball player," I said. "I wanted people to get to know me for who I am, not for what I can do."

During my college career, I grew to understand that my world was larger than just basketball. I intentionally made friends outside of my basketball team. Campus Crusade, Fellowship of Christian Athletes, and Wesley Foundation became a support system for me, a family away from home. Campus Crusade encouraged Christian students to share our faith, removing our focus from ourselves to others. FCA taught us how to be role models off the court, as well as on the court. The Wesley Foundation helped us learn how to build relationships and do life with other believers.

After that day, my Christian friends came to games. Knowing they were there just for me, holding up signs, cheering for me filled me with a new sense of support. It really energized me on the court and built my confidence.

AIA-AUSTRALIA

I noticed a little redheaded girl staring at me wide-eyed. As we filed by her, I looked into her eyes. Playfully, I growled, and she drew back in fear. I had joined the summer AIA Women's 1990 team, which was due to play in Australia.

We were dressed in matching blue sweats and proudly marched into the gym. This was the day we'd be assigned to a host family. Uneasy thoughts floated through my mind. Although I was a racial minority within the AIA team, I didn't know how I would be received in a foreign country. What would the assigned family think of me? What stereotypes filled their thinking? I wanted a welcoming family! The families filled one side of the gym, and our team stood on the other.

Each player's name was called out with the name of their matching family. When my name was called, I finally met my host family. Ironically, it was Red Head's family. They welcomed me, and all my fears went away. We got into their square white van—the mom, the dad, the ten-year-old girl, an eight-year-old boy, and five-year-old Red Head.

The trip was quiet and awkward until Red Head touched my hair and said, "Your hair's fake!"

I touched her hair and told her, "Well, your hair is fake, too!"

Everybody laughed, and that broke the silence. Later I found out that little Red Head had never seen a black person before, so her initial fear of me was understandable.

We arrived at their home where the mom had prepared a meal for us. This was my first experience eating lamb. After filling our plates, everyone sat silently, not eating, but staring at me. I finally realized the guest needed to start eating first. I took a bite of lamb, which I liked, and conversation mercifully came easier. After traveling in Europe and South America in previous summers, it was a relief to be in a country where we spoke the same language.

My summer with AIA, playing basketball, but with a godly focus, earning the right to share the gospel, improved my game. I relaxed and played with a growing confidence. Winning wasn't the focus, but competing was still legitimate. We weren't heading toward a tournament or championship. Each game was a stand-alone event, a platform for us to share the gospel.

Because the exhibition games were close by, the host families came to watch us play. We had our first fan club. Our fans invited others to come see us, as well, including unbelieving friends. The hosts were Christians and knew we'd be sharing the gospel. This kind of support helped us play even better.

During the week I stayed with "my family," we became close. Strangeness melted away, as we grew to care about each other. The mom grew comfortable with me and shared about her life. The ten-year-old girl had just returned from America in a gymnastics competition, so we had lots to talk about. Whenever we were both home, she followed me into my room and visited. Every morning around 5 a.m., I heard the three kids outside my bedroom door, loudly wondering when I was getting up. As I went down the hall to the bathroom, all three children were on my heels. The whole week I was in their home, the children followed me everywhere. When I finally left their home, it was like leaving family.

FINAL YEAR AS A LADY RAIDER

Going into my fifth year, 1990-1991, I was the only one left from my recruitment class. I began to understand and embrace my position as a leader. Because of my experience, I could mentor the younger players, and I wanted to do that. The newer players looked up to me. Even the coaches respected me. In fact, if a recruit considering Texas Tech visited the school, and they professed to be a Christian, they asked me to represent Texas Tech to the newcomer in a positive light.

Rivalry between the University of Texas (UT) Longhorns and Texas Tech (TTU) Lady Raiders had a rich history. The Longhorns vs Lady Raiders' rivalry was well-known throughout Texas, which made the games intense and exciting, but somewhat predictable. From 1977 to 1991 the Longhorns beat the Lady Raiders every single time.

UT was known for its aggressive, dominating players. They had a reputation of being fundamentally sound, a national powerhouse. Everyone respected them, but everybody wanted to beat them.

When the Lady Raiders played Longhorns, it was a true David and Goliath moment. However, the Lady Raiders had experienced an extraordinarily successful season. In the Southwest Conference tournament at SMU (Southern Methodist University), we won the first round. Our next game was against UT. Although we had already lost to them twice that year, on tournament day, I somehow knew we were the team to beat.

I confidently jogged out to the court with my team, and something was just different. Our team's hard work undergirded my peace.

c. 1991. Alexis listening to Texas Tech Coach Sharp's voice.

"Lex," Coach Sharp called, "you're going to have a good game!"

That's all I needed to hear from her. These words empowered me to approach this Southwest Conference tournament game with confidence. She made me feel like a million dollars! Her belief in me made me feel valued and worthy as a player and a person.

Coach also told me, "You're going to score 12 points!"

This comment gave me freedom to play the game

without hesitation or second guessing. Her words brought me life.

"The tongue has the power of life and death..." Proverbs 18:21a

Once the game started, we made shots, rebounded, and dived after loose balls. We could do nothing wrong. We played so well the UT team exchanged looks of shock. Their focus was compromised because they were frustrated with each other. This caught everybody off guard. No one was expecting Texas Tech to win since we'd never defeated UT. But that day everything was going right for us.

UT usually slaughtered their opponents. The game became fierce and the score jumped from us, to them, and back again. By half time, fans and coaches knew the teams were equally matched. Toward the end of the second half, although both sides fought fearlessly, the game stayed close.

Near the end of the game, the Lady Raiders realized we could win. Everybody, players, coaching staff, and fans were on their feet, screaming. UT couldn't pull ahead. This was devastating for them, and they exchanged dazed looks around the court. When the buzzer sounded, the Texas Tech Lady Raiders were victorious over the University of Texas for the first time: 63-61! This made us eligible to play in the finals of the NCAA conference tournament.

The celebration was electric! Everyone was jumping up and down, hugging each other, screaming and laughing, as if we had won a national championship. The UT/Texas Tech curse was broken. We made history for Texas Tech by beating our arch rival. Later Coach said that win was one of the biggest highlights of her entire coaching career.

And, by the way, I scored 12 points, just as Coach predicted.

My final season of Texas Tech basketball ended with a loss during the first round of the NCAA tournament. Even though we lost, it was still an honor to make it that far, and our victory over UT was still ringing in our ears. Finally, we had taken down the giant!

During my years at Texas Tech, the Lady Raiders enjoyed a special run. There was a marked increase in fans showing up to see Tech beat other teams. The risk Texas Tech took on me brought a blessing to the team, the school, the coach, and to me. In the past, Tech had had star players, but this was an all-star team, and I was allowed to participate in their success.

c. 1995. Left to right: Alexis Ware, Texas Tech Coach Marsha Sharp, and Reena Lynch. Texas Tech Women's Basketball Reunion.

CHAPTER 6

CHANGING SEASONS

AGAINST ALL ODDS

"I'll bet you $100 Alexis Ware will never graduate from college!"

A well-known Victoria Advocate sports writer challenged Coach Lahodny when she spoke to him about me. He had written many glowing articles about my high school basketball games, but because he knew I bombed the SAT test, he assumed I wasn't fit for college. He had no confidence in me. Coach disagreed and defended me. I was overjoyed to see him lose that bet.

c. 1991. Alexis graduated from Texas Tech.

Growing up, my mom encouraged all of us to finish high school, but college seemed out of reach. Since I was the first in my family to receive a college degree, most of them drove up to Lubbock, nine and a half hours, to watch me graduate from Texas Tech. Because I went beyond the usual goal of high school, it was a victory for my whole family. I felt so loved, proud, and happy at being able to share this "win" with my family.

At Texas Tech, graduations happen in the departments of your major. My degree was in Human Development and Family Studies, with a minor in Social Work and a certificate in Substance Abuse. My ceremony was in the Human Development building. Hundreds graduated with me that day. Because my last name was Ware, I was near the end.

When I heard, "Alexis Ware" announced by the Texas Tech President, I walked toward him grinning exuberantly. He knew me from our conversation about quitting after my fourth year. That day, he gestured with his hands, shooting a basketball, showing he was proud of me. My family and the rest of the audience cheered when I received my diploma. For the first time, I believed I was a champion off the court. My heart was full and overflowing as I crossed the stage, basking in the approval and pride of my family. Finished!

During my college career, I was never on academic probation and never once doubted that I would graduate. This moment marked the culmination of a long season of growing in the Lord, maturing and learning outside and inside a classroom.

When I finally heard about that newspaperman's bet, I was initially offended, but that quickly was followed by a sense of accomplishment. How grateful I was that those words hadn't been bouncing around in my head before this grand day of graduation. I was overcome with humility, realizing how far the Lord had brought me against all odds.

I was so grateful that I hadn't missed the final year as a Lady Raider and got to be part of the downfall of UT. That final year healed a lot within me. Basketball ended in March, so I still had April and May to finish up my degree. Now what was next?

My basketball career was finished. I intended to never play again. I was basketballed out! Turning in all my gear, I had my teammates sign my shoes and walked away from the sport. Or, so I thought.

DECISIONS, DECISIONS

Panic set in. Everything was changing. Everything was unknown. My friends were entering the workforce, walking confidently into careers. I'd been so focused on basketball, that I gave no thought about what happened after basketball. I needed to find something and fast. Frantically, I searched for my next step. Since I'd been an active participant in Campus Crusade for Christ, and I loved it so much, I applied to them for a ministry position. However, when the rejection letter arrived, I was shocked and disappointed. Any kind of rejection threw me back into the familiar feelings of worthlessness and insecurity. I wanted a solid future, not a future of question marks and uncertainty.

However, I got a call from Athletes-In-Action (ironically, a branch of Campus Crusade) to play on their fall exhibition basketball team. This wasn't the same AIA team I'd played with during the summers. This team was hand-selected and made up of Division I elite athletes.

My initial response was "No." I was finished with basketball. My shoes were signed. I was done. Done!

They called me several more times, trying to convince me I'd benefit by taking part. They explained that the real purpose of this team was saving lives through the language of basketball, and the purpose of our games was just a platform for presenting the gospel. Although the skill of basketball was important, we weren't playing for a championship. We needed to perform well so the audience would listen to our gospel message. The coach's job was not on the line, the players didn't have to fear losing scholarships, and there weren't any trophies coming. Knowing we wouldn't be penalized by the coach every time we made a mistake, there was just an atmosphere of freedom and encouragement on and off the court.

This was indeed ministry. That appealed to me. This might be an incredible opportunity. Yet, because I was graduating from college and all the other graduates were moving into adult jobs, it seemed I should, too. AIA wasn't a job, and there was no paycheck. They would pay all my expenses, but again I'd come home with no paycheck—just a once-in-a-lifetime experiences, memories and eternal fruit.

While I was still in college, my parents were supportive when I had to ask people for support in order to participate in AIA. But now that I had finished my degree, they didn't understand the concept of still raising money. They were ready to see me earn a full living.

"You have an education," Mom said. "Don't be going outside of the family asking for money."

I wrote her a long letter, not asking her to make my decision, but rather to support whatever I decided. As the letter formed on the page, the answer became clear. God was showing me my next step.

LETTER TO MOM

Mom,

I'm sure you know or have an idea why I'm writing you. Well, I'm not writing to make you change your mind about Athletes in Action. I am writing you to let you know that I love you and I wouldn't do anything to hurt you. I've been a Christian since the 10th grade but I really didn't know the true meaning of Christianity till college. During my five years in college, God helped me to depend more and more upon Him each day. I'm not saying I've done it each day, but I learn more and more that He's all I need. He's the only one who will be there when I need Him at any time.

For the past year, I've had a very hard time giving all my worries to God. I've spent many nights crying because I wasn't sure what I needed to do after college. My prayer partner and I have been praying that God would show me what I'm supposed to be doing. Since March of this year, I was almost sure that it was God's will for me to go to graduate school. This was the last thing I wanted to do. It seemed God was telling me to go to grad school. So, I really thought I had everything planned out. I remember AIA asking, before school was out, if I wanted to travel with them in the fall; I said "no" because I thought it was time for me to start working or start school in the fall. At this point in time, I totally blocked AIA out of the picture. I was going to have to raise more money monthly. I didn't feel comfortable doing that two times in a row.

So, my plan was to go to school and work. Well, two weeks ago I remember telling my prayer partner that I wished I could take a break from school in the fall. I thought maybe I could find a job. I haven't heard from anyone yet. I was getting frustrated because I didn't understand why God hadn't allowed me to find a job. Also, why the graduate school course from North Texas didn't match up with Tech's courses. So, I mailed Tech's grad book to North Texas so the advisor could point out the classes that would transfer. While I'm having second thoughts about what I was planning on doing in the fall, I got this call two Thursdays ago from AIA. I told her that I didn't know if I wanted to do it because I wanted to work and go to school. She said to pray about it and she'll call me later. Well, Mom, I definitely felt like this was a door opener for me. Ever since I got that call, I was wondering if God was trying to tell me something. I wondered if He was trying to tell me to do mission work. To be honest with you, I love doing mission work. I feel like I have a big opportunity to share what God is doing and has done for me in my life.

I worry at times because I'm not sure what I want right now. I do know that I don't want to go to grad school this fall because I really would like to take a break before starting something new. I'm very burned out from school. I'm barely making it this summer.

Anyway, this past weekend I went to a church retreat for college students. I really learned a lot. I prayed and prayed trying to see what God wants me to do. One speaker talked about how God just wants us to let go of ALL our worries and give it to Him. That He will take care of His children as He said He would. Also, he talked about us saying, "What if?" or "If only. . ." Well, in God's eyes there is no such thing. Everything that has happened and will happen is all in God's plan. We do have a choice, but we can't do it by ourselves. Something I realize after looking back on the retreat is everyone has decisions to make. Whatever the decisions will be, God will not leave that person in the dark should it be a wrong decision. I said I wanted to do what God wants me to do. I don't know what He wants me to do. It could be to go to work, school, or AIA. I'm not sure. I'm having a hard time right now. I spend sleepless nights because I'm confused.

I'm, still looking for work here in Lubbock. I realize that I've done a lot of traveling—I love it. I also realize that one of these days I will have to settle down and make a living. Again, I feel like another door is open and I will have an opportunity to play ball once more before it's all said and done. But I'm clueless. I just wish that you all would try to understand—not agree—with the way I feel, and why I feel like this. My goal in life is to do what God wants me to do. I can't go wrong if I follow Him. As it says in the Bible, "All things work together for the good of those who love the Lord." I truly believe this because God has brought me through some rough times. When I say rough times, I mean school, basketball and my friends. I had a very hard time this past year because most all my friends graduated last year. I had to make new friendships and it was hard, but I made some.

Anyway, I love you and I want you to know I don't want to hurt anyone in making decisions in my life.

Take care,

Sissy

P.S. Thanks for your concern about my future. I wish I could get married, and I wouldn't have to worry about these decisions. Ha ha ha!

By the end of the letter, it became clear that a job was out of the question, grad school seemed like drudgery, and AIA meant I could stay longer with my beloved basketball. I wanted to travel to speak to more people about the Lord. For the first time I realized, that above all, my future needed to invest in serving the Lord, however that looks. That became my number one priority. After rereading that letter, I realized God had made my path straight. Straight to AIA!

"Trust in the Lord with all your heart and lean not on your own understanding; in all your ways submit to him, and he will make your paths straight." Proverbs 3:5-6

CHAPTER 7

KIDS ACROSS AMERICA

FRAGMENTED SCHEDULE

The decision to play basketball for AIA meant I needed several jobs because the AIA team only played in November and December. To fill my year, I became a substitute teacher in Victoria, Texas during January through May, director of Kids Across America (KAA) Camp during the summer, and a basketball player with AIA during November and December. For the next few years, my life was full and varied.

CAMP

"What would you do if a kid hit you?" This strange question confused me. The Director of KAA asked me this very odd question at the beginning of my interview.

Nervously laughing, I responded, "I'd hit them back!"

Thankfully, the Director laughed with me, understanding that I was just kidding.

My friend from college, Robyn, recommended that I apply for a summer position with Kanakuk, a Christian sports camp in Branson, Missouri.

Kids from all over the US came to Kanakuk to improve their sport skills and to grow in their relationship with the Lord. I realized I could still combine ministry with sports, so I applied and was granted a telephone interview. Her question about hitting seemed out of place, considering the campers come from suburban America. But that slid into the background of my mind when I was offered the job on the spot. My contract came in the mail, so I filled it out and made the flight to Missouri. It was my first job after graduating from college.

They picked me up and took me to the campground. Because I knew no one, was unfamiliar with life in the woods, and was unsure what they expected, I was anxious. Whispering arrow prayers to the Lord, I needed to remember He had brought me here. He could be trusted, and my confidence was in Him and nothing else.

At the camp, however, I realized the campers weren't from suburban America. These were inner city kids. Something was off.

"This isn't the camp I interviewed for!" I said. Now I understood her earlier confusing question.

The director said, "This is where we need you."

1991 was the first year for Kids Across America (KAA), an inner city camp for urban youth in Golden, Missouri. The camp was located on a mountain top, surrounded by 240 acres of wilderness and bordered by Table Rock Lake. This set the scene for sports and quiet times with God. Twelve new and spacious cabins containing bunk beds could sleep a dozen. Each cabin contained a bathroom and a window fan. They were surrounded by clearings for tennis courts, football/soccer field, basketball court and a large gym which held the promise of healthy future competitions. A strong sense of peace covered the entire place.

I was still nervous, but I immediately went into work mode. Drawing on a few college experiences where I worked briefly with kids, I faced this new challenge with excitement.

Inner city kids? Just what did that mean? I needed to confront my own prejudices, expectations and fears that week as

I became acquainted with the kids. I had no previous experience with urban youth, so I battled preconceived ideas from TV. Maybe I'd get beat up, or they'd have weapons, or they were all criminals.

Eventually, as I grew to know the kids, I saw that my first fears were groundless. I found fatherless boys, desperately needing a man to teach them how to be a man. Fatherless girls sought male attention of any kind. Kids, who lived in a world where the government provided for them, came with the attitude that all things would just come to them. I saw broken hearts as many of the kids didn't know how to navigate through life. Emotions overrode reason. Their need for love and the Lord overwhelmed me.

REPRODUCING REPRODUCERS

The KAA camp counselors were athletic Christian college students from across the U.S. They were handpicked and recruited from various colleges and backgrounds. They had to be believers in Christ, athletic, have a heart for youth, and be willing to cross cultural lines. The pay was low, so this ministry required an eternal motive.

Bruce Morgan, the Executive Director, encouraged us to "Reproduce reproducers!"

> **"...go and make disciples of all nations...teaching them everything I have commanded you...Surely, I am with you always." Matthew 28:19**

This verse provided the foundation for the concept of learning, obeying, teaching, passing on what we had been given ourselves. We were given tools designed to help us give truth to someone else, through specific spiritual disciplines: having a quiet time, praying, and meditating. Having practiced these habits for years, when I was given the opportunity to teach, I spoke from experience.

TRAINING COUNSELORS

"I don't want to go to my director because of you!" I said to a girl in my cabin. "It'll make me look like I don't know what I'm doing. That would be embarrassing. We're like your family away from home! We need to live like a family."

I didn't want my director to think I couldn't handle the job. Because I came to KAA straight from college, I didn't have the necessary skills for working with kids. My first experience as a counselor meant I would stay in a cabin with two other counselors and ten girl campers. We had to learn how to communicate with each other. Living with the kids differed from having a college roommate.

I appealed to the new campers to act like a family, even though many of them had little to no experience with a healthy family unit. I respected them, and they respected me. From what little I knew, most of these urban campers came from difficult backgrounds in which there was little to no respect being displayed or honored.

That summer at KAA was my first time to be in close community with "inner city youth." The days moved into weeks, and I heard from girls, having to raise themselves and siblings, facing abuses at home and being uncertain of even having a home. As I addressed their sometimes-disrespectful behavior, I began to see behind it, to the true issues that might be causing them to respond like that. I knew I was just where God wanted me to be. A new heart was emerging from me. A peculiar love began to develop. I discovered I had compassion for people in pain.

Sometimes these college students serving as counselors came with misconceptions (just like I did), making wrong assumptions about the campers. Some counselors came with an untried work ethic and had to be encouraged to find pleasure in doing a task well. A few came to camp while their parents were divorcing at home, making their own futures vague. During their time at camp, they were encouraged by the leadership in their personal walk with the Lord. As the counselors served that summer, they were learning, too.

The first few days, I was still thinking I'd rather be at Kanakuk, than KAA. Robyn, who had recommended that I apply for Kanakuk, had painted such a great picture of the sports aspects and that appealed to me. However, the inner city kids gravitated to me, and it seemed we'd known each other for years. It was the campers at KAA who changed my mind. Every day, as we worked, cleaned, and shared meals together, the bond grew more intense, especially through Bible study. As I submitted to God's obvious will for me, I released those thoughts of changing camps and never visited them again. I was home.

Each group of kids spent sixteen days at camp. At this early point in the development of camp, there were no guidelines or consequences for the campers. As things happened, rules were developed. Each infraction required that we as a staff think through a proper response and consequence.

Counselors were required to oversee the kids in their cabins. Plastic shower curtains divided the showers and gave some privacy between commodes. Large window fans provided the only air-conditioning. Even though the cabins were primitive, we encouraged the girls to take care of the cabin and their own stuff. Each girl had a different daily job assignment (clean the shower, sweep/mop the floor, clean the toilets, etc.)

As the days unfolded, we saw many inappropriate actions such as refusing to clean up their part of the cabin, being disrespectful to a counselor or each other, using profanity, or refusing to take part in activities. Addressing these behaviors one-on-one became part of the job of the counselor.

I saw that the KAA staff were working from a one-mind environment, meaning our daily routine focused us on Jesus. Every song we sang focused us. Our time alone in the Bible focused us. The sports activities brought us to a Jesus focus. Prayer punctuated every day as we prayed before and after each activity and meal. Even when frustrated, we learned to address it through scripture. For example, when frustrations turned to anger, the counselors went to the Word and found:

> **". . .human anger does not produce the righteousness that God desires." James 1:20**

At the end of the first summer, the Lord humbled me by making me realize I had initially put myself above the campers by being judgmental. I wasn't seeing them as the Lord saw them, children of value and beauty. Although I hadn't experienced the things these kids had gone through, they could sense I had tremendous empathy for them. I grew to love them as I got to know them.

A DAY IN THE LIFE OF A CAMPER

"Girls, it's time to clean up the cabin," Kelandria, the counselor said. "Everybody needs pitch in."

"I don't have to do that! Nobody can tell me what to do!" she said defiantly.

"D'Nae, you need to clean, too," said Kelandria. "The sooner we get through, the sooner we can get into our activity. You're holding up the whole cabin."

"You—, I told you no one can make me do a—thing! I don't give a—. Just try to make me!" D'Nae folded her hands across her chest, took a threatening stance, and stared defiantly at her counselor.

Her counselor described her as "A mouthy, outspoken, lip-smacking, eye-rolling, dismissive pre-teen who was determined to be heard."

Sometimes our campers came from such difficult circumstances they were ready to fight anytime. They lived in a defensive mode. D'Nae saw her counselor and the rules as an insult to her own power, and she wouldn't give in.

"I hate this—camp! Wish I'd never come. I just don't care," she said.

One day, everyone had all they could take from D'Nae, so she was required to run the hill. When a camper messed up, they had to run the steep hill on the campground at 6 a.m. before everyone else got up. However, they didn't run it alone. Their cabin counselor got up and ran it with them. This was humbling to see their counselor, who did nothing wrong, being punished with them. The camper saw first hand that an innocent person also took their consequence, just as Jesus did for us. Also, it modeled that whenever we make poor choices and face discipline, we never face it alone. This picture of Jesus' sacrifice for us was permanently etched in the campers' minds.

At 6:00 a.m., Kelandria tried to wake D'Nae, but she mumbled, "No! I'm not doing it."

After some back and forth, D'Nae was removed from her bed bodily by all three counselors. They put her shoes on, tied them and Kelandria and D'Nae went out the door to run.

"This is stupid," she mumbled.

Kelandria was hoping to run to the top of the hill, then slow down on the way back and talk with her, but that's not what happened.

D'Nae was disobedient and out of control, but she could run. Although Kelandria was extremely athletic, she ran up the hill with her, neck-and-neck. However, when they reached the top, Kelandria was over-heated from running that steep hill. D'Nae turned and ran down the hill toward camp. She wasn't breathing hard, but the counselor could barely talk. Later Kelandria learned that D'Nae was on the track team at her school. The planned conversation never happened. Over the course of the week, Kelandria spent deliberate time with D'Nae and tried to help her understand the bigger picture: God loves her and God has a plan for her life. Being at this camp was part of that plan and God wanted a relationship with her. These truth messages bombarded D'Nae at every turn, but she responded better to men staffers than women. We saw her talking intently with a couple of the men staffers.

She was a difficult camper but over three years, D'Nae went from being a defiant young girl to being offered a place in the Higher Ground camp, where only the best leaders, the most committed Christians are invited so they can be exposed to deeper teaching. While she was there, leaders discovered that D'Nae had been busy organizing various ministries at her church back home. What a turnaround!

The counselors loved these kids unconditionally throughout each day. The hours were long. Counselors woke before the campers to have a 6:00 a.m. Bible study/quiet time. At 7:30, they awakened the kids, encouraged them to get dressed for the day, and clean up the cabin. Everyone went to breakfast in the dining hall, returned to their cabins and participated in a Bible study/quiet time. After this, campers attended three consecutive activities taught by the counselors. Counselors and campers came back together for each meal. After lunch, everyone was required to take part in FOB (Flat On Back!) for a short rest period. More activities in the afternoon were followed by an hour of free time, during which the campers could choose their own sport. Because all the other activities were boys-with-boys or girls-with-girls, free time was the only mingling time of day for the kids under the watchful eyes of staff.

Often at the term's end, counselors and kids would both be in tears. The counselors, who grew to love the kids, knew some kids were walking back into difficult home situations. Kids didn't want to go home but wanted to stay in the encouraging sanctuary of camp. We all realized that KAA had become a place of refuge, acceptance, love, and freedom.

I remember one girl telling me tearfully, "I want to stay. I love it here. We get to learn about Jesus, we're treated well and we get three meals a day!"

KAA was a summer job, but my heart had been pierced with a deep love for these kids. When I witnessed the changes in their lives that could happen in a short time, I began to understand that God was at work in this environment and I wanted to be part of it. As I watched Him soften their hard hearts, free campers from their past and circumstances, I changed too. My concept of God was enlarging. I was excited to share with them the security of living for God.

CHAPTER 8

AIA-TRAINING WITH A PURPOSE

WATER AND FEAR

"Man!" I said. "I don't know if I can handle getting in all this water."

Looking at the river rapids, my fear increased. I didn't want to do whitewater rafting.

After working at KAA for the summer in Golden, Missouri, I rested a month at home before joining Athletes In Action in Ohio for training camp. The AIA team trained in October and toured in November. Because AIA started each fall with an almost brand new team, every year we had to rebuild ourselves to be a solid squad of men and women. After weeks of onsite training in Ohio, we drove to Pocono, Pennsylvania, for whitewater rafting on the Lehigh River, this year's team-building activity. Twelve women, fourteen men, and staff wearing matching red AIA t-shirts walked toward the rafts on a beautiful sunny day.

Immediately, I was afraid because I didn't know how to swim.

Each raft would have a guide who told us what to do so we wouldn't turn over. The guide explained about wearing life jackets, but I didn't trust a life jacket. I put it on because I didn't want to be the only one not doing it. I was beyond scared; I was terrified.

Since we were athletes, they assigned us to the most difficult route which meant more danger. Boarding the raft, the guide told us to sit on the edge, with our feet dangling inside. I did that, and we began to float. The instability of floating unnerved me.

I told my raftmates, "Now listen to the guide!"

The guide said, "If you fall out of the raft, just lay back, and let the water take you down the river."

I prayed, "There's no way I can just let the water take me. Lord, please help me not to fall out."

We shoved off, entered the river and moved ahead. The water was calm, the ride was smooth, the sun was warm, and I knew I was safe. But then, a turn in the river revealed rapids. Now I knew why they called it whitewater rafting. The water churned so violently, that it became white as it was thrown into the air. Our raft picked up speed, and we rushed down the river. Although we were told to sit on the side of the raft, I repositioned myself to be inside the raft.

I repeated directions from the guide in a really loud voice. Everyone needed to hear what she said.

She shouted, "Paddle hard."

I shouted, "PADDLE HARD! PADDLE HARD!"

She shouted, "Lean left!"

"LEAN LEFT! LEAN LEFT!"

She shouted, "Paddle forward!"

"PADDLE FORWARD, PADDLE FORWARD!"

I didn't care if I got on their nerves, I needed to be sure my raftmates heard everything the guide said because I didn't want to flip over.

The river took another severe turn, and we were swirling in a place of calm again. My fear subsided, and I rejoined the rest of the team sitting on the side of the raft. I could breathe again.

c. 1993. As a team building exercise, the Athletes in Action team floated the Lehigh River, PA. Alexis is on the far side, middle. Notice the person in the water.

Peace was all around. But not for long. The peaceful interlude ended when the next turn put us square in the whitewater again.

Up and down, up and down, up and down, the river left me terrified and hovering inside the raft again. This was the pattern for the trip until almost the end. My feelings bounced between peacefulness and panic.

Near the end of our ride, our guide yelled above the roaring water, "There's going to be a big drop. Once you drop, make sure you don't stop paddling. Make sure you don't celebrate too soon!"

I understood the importance of not celebrating too soon. This eight-foot drop was called "The Grand Finale Falls."

Drop? Drop? What did she mean drop?

All I could think was, "We're going to die."

My strategy was to watch a raft in front of us to tell when the water would get rough. My eyes were firmly affixed on that front raft. When they disappeared, I knew what was coming. Their raft dropped out of sight. My heart sank, and fear overwhelmed me. Because they didn't do what they were told, they tipped over.

"Oh," I thought, "We're going to die for sure!"

When we took the drop, I shrieked at the top of my lungs, "PADDLE! PADDLE! PADDLE! PADDLE!"

I was going crazy! Our raft took a severe downturn, and my stomach was in my throat, but my mouth was screaming. Horror seized me completely. For those two seconds, I experienced terror as never before.

We hit white water at the base of the falls and paddled frantically. Sure enough, our raft righted itself, and we didn't turn over. Thank the Lord!

We finished the ride uneventfully. I calmed down, shocked that I'd done this and survived. The fear that had overtaken me just a few minutes before transformed into a pride that I had done it. I'd never have chosen to go whitewater rafting on my own, and I'm so glad I did it, but I'll never do it again.

Facing my fear of water taught me who to believe. In this case, the guide in my raft knew the truth about the river and how to handle it. Because I trusted her, I listened and followed her commands.

When we took the drop, I screamed, "PADDLE! PADDLE!"

I wasn't speaking out of my experience, but hers, and I trusted her. When we experience frightful things in this life, we need to figure out who is our guide. Someone with experience and success. Someone who has "Been there, done that." Choosing the wrong guide can land you in big trouble.

In my life, I choose Jesus as my guide.

"My sheep listen to my voice; I know them, and they follow me." John 10:27

WAR AND TRUST 1992

Shock and betrayal registered on my partner's face as I shot him in the chest with a bright red paintball, signaling he was dead and out of the game. Everyone stood stunned, jaws dropped. My partner looked at me with disbelief. He couldn't believe I betrayed him. I turned away and looked at the other girl, waiting for her to shoot her partner, but she just couldn't. So I did! Red paint ran down his jacket as he looked at me in shock. All I could do was grin.

To become a successful unit and function as a team, AIA provided an intense training camp for both women and men. Like the whitewater rafting trip the previous year, everything we did pointed to a greater truth. This month-long training camp in October 1992 was built around a war scenario using paint balls; the goal was always to capture a flag from the opponent's territory. We were taken out to a dense forest. Because it was fall, a thick blanket of leaves covered the ground. We were instructed to layer our clothes because paint balls can hurt. A helmet protected our heads, with shields to protect our faces.

Each woman was given a male partner, and the partners were assigned to one of two teams. Each person was given a paint ball gun, and each team used a different color of paint. Strategy, trusting teammates, and shouted warnings unified all the teams as they tried to shoot paintballs at each other. If you were shot, you were "dead." The games were divided up into rounds. On Round One, I was hit square between the eyes, splattering bright yellow paint all over my face shield. The battles were wild, violent, and colorful.

Each team strategized about how to capture the flag and conquer the other team. Some teammates hid under the leaves; others hid behind trees. Adrenalin ruled as we tried to win because we were, after all, competitive athletes. This was like a real war. I loved it!

On the last round of fighting, the leaders asked the women to meet with them. They gave us instructions to "kill" our partners when the signal was given. My friend was dating her partner. Many of the girls disagreed with the instructor, not wanting to "shoot" their teammates, but that didn't change our assignment. As we walked back to rejoin our partners, many women were conflicted. Everyone took their positions, guys flat on the ground, girls squatting behind a tree. I wasn't attached to my partner, so when the signal was given, I turned and shot him. Everyone stared at me in shock. My friend and I exchanged glances, she shook her head indicating she couldn't shoot her partner, so I took aim and splattered red paint all over him too. The two guys stared up at me in total disbelief. In my mind, I was obeying the rules, even the new ones. In theirs, I had betrayed my team.

The walk back to the meeting site was quiet as everyone tried to process what had just happened. Comments from the guys revealed their disappointment, broken trust, betrayal, anger, frustration, and confusion. Some girls thought the request to kill the partners wasn't fair. Others decided they needed to obey and accomplished the mission. (That was me!) The whole exercise created brief animosity amongst the group, but was soon dissolved, realizing the lesson was clear.

The lesson: God's Word says,

> **"Be alert and of sober mind. Your enemy the devil prowls around like a roaring lion looking for someone to devour." I Peter 5:8**

Stay on your guard. Your enemy comes at you from all angles. Stay alert. Be careful who you trust.

I'll never forget those lessons from that game.

This experience gave me a sense of fighting a real battle as a Christian. My battles rage mostly in my mind, so that's where

I had to decide about my behavior, my words, my responses. I learned from others when I saw them struggling to get out of a trap. I knew not to go there. When we "betrayed" our partners, I realized in the larger sense, we must put our total trust in Jesus alone, not in other people. In the battle, the adrenalin caused us to maintain a hyper-awareness of all our surroundings. In the battle of the every day, we needed to stay alert and not swayed. Occasionally, our earthly decisions rub people the wrong way. We are called to expect persecution or misunderstanding, sometimes from those closest to us. Often this response comes when others do not grasp the big picture, just as my teammates held resentment to those who were following orders.

MORE THAN A GAME

Whenever we traveled and pulled into a restaurant, the AIA black, red and yellow bus drew attention. The bus looked like it carried celebrities, so curious people approached us. They wondered who we were, especially since we wore identical blue warm-ups. Sometimes, people asked for a tour of the bus. They were stunned when they saw a table, beds, a kitchen, and 2 tv's. It was a very nice living room. Because they were receptive, the door was open to share the gospel, our testimonies, and our team brochures.

Until now my involvement with AIA had been in summers while I was attending Texas Tech. The fall team was formed by invitation only. Many were All-American players. What an honor to play with some of the greatest women basketball players!

Because of the elite level of each teammate, our practices at training camp were intense. Every player was an expert and had the potential to be a starter. After camp, I became the starting point guard, a choice that humbled and pleased me. As I met with my team, I realized I could still be a leader, even with these star athletes. After a month of training camp, we travelled as an exhibition team, playing top Division I college teams across America.

Before the Women's National Basketball Association (WNBA) existed, we got the attention of those who enjoyed women's basketball. We didn't realize we attracted so much attention. We never considered we'd be treated like celebrities—autographs and all! When we played, our agenda was to share the gospel and play exceptional basketball. The agenda of the college teams was to sharpen their skills before their upcoming season.

Winning souls to Christ was more important than winning basketball games. At each game, before half-time, local Campus Crusade for Christ staff and volunteers passed out AIA brochures which highlighted the teammates and the gospel. At half-time, we took turns sharing our personal testimonies. Because there were Campus Crusade staffs in each location, those who responded were left in their care.

We needed to be legitimately competitive with the teams on the court. It was customary for the AIA team to share lunch with the opposing team, visiting with them as friends, rather than opponents. Afterward, one or two of our players shared their personal testimony and the gospel. This spawned respect between the teams. But, when it was game time, the competition was on. If not, the audience wouldn't pay attention and listen to our gospel message. We won 75% of our games, a record that earned us respect.

AIA played University of Tennessee, University of Texas, Texas Tech, University of Southern California, and other successful college teams. Then we came against University of Connecticut (UConn), which was developing a reputation of being unstoppable. We didn't stop them either. We lost the game.

Because we interacted pre-game with the UConn team over lunch and shared our testimonies, one of the UConn players asked us to pray for her mom who was battling cancer. Although we never knew the outcome, we were humbled to be asked to pray. There was much more going on than simply a basketball game. We built trust and friendship. Our team walked away from that with a bigger picture of what we were really doing through the avenue of basketball. We all began to grasp our life's mission, and it was bigger than basketball.

For the next four years, I lived the schedule of AIA in the fall, KAA in the summer, substitute teaching the rest of the time.

CHAPTER 9

KAA FAMILY

IS THIS THE END?

"If you don't stop playing basketball, by the time you turn 30 you'll be in a wheelchair."

Wheelchair? The doctor's words shocked me. In my mind, nothing could keep me from playing basketball. I understood the doctor. I needed to stop basketball right away. This was a no-brainer.

I was 27 years old. My diagnosis was degenerative joint disease, which causes inflammation to eat up joint cartilage. My knees hurt all the time. The relentless AIA schedule had taken its toll. The last season we played 20 games in 23 days. Although I was having a blast, I didn't realize how much wear and tear it put on my knees. My mind was in a great place, but my body was weakening.

This diagnosis meant I could never play competitive basketball again. My life and efforts up to then had been focused on the game I now was forbidden to play. Although it was heartbreaking, I prayed for the Lord to show me the next step. Just the next step. By this time, my entire identity was larger than basketball, so I accepted this news with a resolve and peace that surprised even me.

> **"'For I know the plans I have for you,' declares the Lord, 'plans to prosper you and not to harm you, plans to give you hope and a future.'" Jeremiah 29:11**

The following season, AIA didn't have a team director, someone who prepared the way for the team as they traveled from one city or state to the next. I was asked to fill in the gap as a director of that tour. This request came as a surprise. Apprehension overcame my confidence as I thought through the actual position's responsibilities. I was the same age as the players, so why should they listen to me? Their athletic credentials exceeded mine, but I needed to manage them. The AIA staff affirmed my leadership abilities and their support. Because of their confidence in me, I accepted that position for the next season.

Since I'd been a team member, I knew some past difficulties. For example, many times frustration rippled throughout the team when it came time to decide where to eat. I simplified that process by offering them three choices 30 minutes before getting there. The decision was made by the time we arrived, and we quickly ate our meal.

Taken out of the game, I did something I would have never chosen for myself. This was a time for the Lord to develop my administrative skills because I would need them in the future.

ME? DIRECTOR?

After serving as KAA camp counselor in 1991, when I returned in 1992, I was asked to be the assistant director. The following year in 1993, Executive Director Bruce Morgan offered me the director's position at a new KAA-I camp. I immediately recommended someone else.

"God didn't tell me to ask her," he said. "He told me to ask you!"

Shaking inside, I told him I didn't know the Bible well enough, nor did I know how to manage college students or young people. Having never done this before, I didn't want to look incompetent.

"I promise, I'll guide you every step. I won't leave you hanging," he said.

I accepted the position reluctantly, feeling inadequate since I had never been the overseer of anything that big before. Hanging on to Bruce's words, I trusted God to do what He called me to do.

c. 1994. KAA staff dressed up to do a skit. Left to right: Latoya, Leslie, and Alexis

KAA-I was a brand new camp in 1993, and I was the first women's director, partnering with Bruce as men's director. Although Bruce organized and facilitated the staff training, I was in charge of the women counselors. Overseeing the kitchen staff and the office was also part of my responsibility. An intense week of training and building up of staff members prepared us for the summer's work. We knew and trusted each other. My confidence was soaring, and I couldn't wait for the campers to arrive. We focused on the Lord, so when the kids arrived, they found a unified team, fully equipped to reach into the lives of the kids and love them straight to Jesus.

KAA was a place that developed deep friendships that have lasted over the years. For example, the head of my office staff was a college student named Mandisa Hudley. She had a beautiful singing voice, so whenever I spoke to the whole camp, I asked Mandisa to sing first. She was shy and uncertain, but obedient. Everyone loved her voice. This turned into a weekly event. Many years later, Mandisa competed on American Idol placing ninth, which catapulted her to a professional singing career. Today she's been nominated for music awards, including Grammy and Dove Awards. The Lord has used her to minister to people all over the world.

Several years ago, after attending one of her concerts, she stopped signing books to come visit with me and my friends. I thanked her for being so faithful to the Lord for so long.

"No, I need to thank you," Mandisa said. "At KAA, you taught me how to have a quiet time."

God had used me to participate in a kingdom investment!

One week, KAA invited Nicole C. Mullen (now Scott), a Christian singer famous for "My Redeemer Lives," to bring her family to camp to model a whole-family dynamic. As I was playing basketball with some camp boys, Nicole walked up and said, "I want to play, too!"

I looked at her in disbelief and said, "You don't know how to play!"

She laughed and requested, "Come on! You and I will play these boys!"

We played and we won!

After that, we became good friends and still are to this day. Years later, Nicole's successful career was recognized with many awards and a place in the Christian Music Hall of Fame.

SINK OR SWIM

I don't know how to swim. There, I said it. I can run circles around many people on the basketball court, but I never learned how to swim. As Director of KAA, I saw the counselors horsing around a lot near the pool. They just loved pushing each other in.

One day, I saw them push a counselor into the shallow end.

While I was shouting, "Hey! She doesn't know how to..." they pushed ME into the deep end.

As I sank quickly below the surface of the water, fear gripped me, as my legs and arms reacted with instinctive directionless wild swinging. Somehow, I managed to get to the side and get out of the pool. When I got back on solid ground, I firmly walked wordlessly away from the crowd. There was dead silence as they realized with horror just what they had done to their director.

Walking into my cabin, dripping, fuming and shaking, anger overtook my thoughts. I couldn't figure out who to be mad at. I could still feel the out-of-control helplessness of the past few minutes. Finally, calming down and slowing down my thoughts, I realized they just didn't understand.

I stayed in my cabin and didn't come out till breakfast the next morning.

When I entered the dining hall for breakfast, everything stopped. Conversations ceased. There stood my sheepish counselors, holding up big signs saying, "We're sorry," and "We love you."

I smiled and gave them grace. And forgiveness. I recognized they didn't know I couldn't swim. The lesson for the counselors: Don't make a move until you have all the facts.

HIT ME!

"Why are you fighting each other? If you want to hit somebody, HIT ME. HIT ME!"

A couple of counselors had brought two 12-year-old girls to me for discipline. They had been caught viciously fighting with each other. By the time they were standing before me, the anger had turned to fear. I took them into our small windowless room where we speak privately to talk things out. They watched me intently, wondering what I would do or say. When I issued the invitation to hit me, one of the girls pulled back and socked me square in the stomach with her fist. Stunned, everything around us just froze in time. I wasn't prepared at all, so I took the full brunt of the slug.

Coughing a little, I looked at the other girl and asked, "Do you want to hit me, too?"

"Nnnnno, Ma'am!" she mumbled, looking terrified.

"Stop fighting! Go back to your cabin right now."

What I gave to those girls was a picture of God's grace, by not making them face their own earned consequences. What they gave me was the realization that I might be careful what I ask for.

CALLED ONE

KAA required adults to accompany the kids. The adults who brought the kids to camp were called Kaleos, a Greek word for "called one." These adults were leaders or parents who either led programs or otherwise invested in the kids. Because they worked hard to organize and mentor during the school year, they usually showed up at camp in a very ragged state. It is hard work to gather up 75+ kids with all their gear and travel for hours. The camp atmosphere was called "a bubble bath with Jesus." Kaleos were out of their comfort zones, away from responsibility for their campers, becoming saturated with Jesus at every turn. This was a camp within a camp.

A special leader was assigned to oversee just the Kaleos. They took them to their daily activities and Bible study and led them in evening devotionals. Many Kaleos came to camp at the end of their rope, at the end of their hope, visionless. During their time at camp, because the Jesus-focus is so strong, many go home with hope renewed and a new vision. They are able to return to ministry with enthusiasm and passion to continue in their calling. Lifelong friendships can develop. On occasion, some of the Kaleos rededicated their lives to the Lord and His calling on their lives.

A HAVEN

"We—we we. We want the campers! WE—WE WE. WE WANT THE CAMPERS!"

When a busload of kids arrived at KAA, they were welcomed by screaming counselors, banging loudly on the bus, demanding they get off!

This was startling, especially for those kids who'd just spent hours sitting idly on a bus. That initial shock set the tone for what was to come. They were very awake, very aware, and a little scared.

Some campers arrived irritable because they traveled a long distance. They were often afraid of meeting new people or didn't want to be out of their comfort zones. Others arrived excited after waiting all year in anticipation.

Many kids experienced such different lives from what I'd known. God was growing a deep compassion within me, as I desired so much for them. Because the Lord was giving me a new freedom, I wanted to share with the kids how freedom could be theirs, too.

For the campers, KAA was a haven. Because some campers were expected to take adult roles at home, at KAA, they could just be kids, have fun, and do various activities. They were exposed to swimming, sailing, canoeing, skiing, tubing, rock climbing, basketball, football, golf, volleyball, archery, high element ropes course and more. Through these activities, daily Bible studies and an occasional evening party, the kids were constantly given encouragement and the gospel. Every activity pointed to conquering fears, team building, to faith in God, and other lessons for life. Always, Jesus was the focus. At the midpoint of each camping week, we dramatized the crucifixion which revealed what Jesus had done for them. For the first time, they could SEE the sacrifice of Jesus dying to take the punishment for their sins. For many, this was a hinge for their lives, life before Jesus and life after Jesus. Many left KAA with a new commitment to the Lord, a new direction for their lives and a firm foundation. They grasped God was with them, and He had a plan for their lives bigger than their situation.

RACHEL

"One of these days," I said, "I want you to take my spot at KAA as the women's director."

Rachel Wingfield stood in stunned silence.

She'd come to camp when she was sixteen years old. I saw her leadership ability and character to back it up with dependability, integrity, maturity and willingness to go above and beyond what was asked. She cared deeply about people. I watched her make time for those who needed to talk through issues. Above all, she was teachable. The Lord prompted me to do for her what had been done for me; to believe in her even if she didn't believe in herself.

Upon graduating from high school, Rachel served as a college counselor for KAA. Fast forward five years. Rachel had now graduated from college and was offered the directorship of KAA. She did, indeed, take my spot.

Today, Rachel, a wife and mother, is the executive director of a non-profit in Louisiana where she helps others minister to the poor. She says, "The way Alexis poured into me is how I now pour into others."

Over the years, I was privileged to see several other kids come as campers and return several years later as staffers. Reproducing reproducers!

DIRECTOR SPEAK

Early on, Bruce, the executive director told me, "Alexis, you need to speak to the whole camp."

"Oh no," I said. "There are plenty of others who can speak."

"The campers need to hear from you," he said. "You're the women's director."

Sharing my testimony through AIA was one thing but assembling a God-message for hundreds of people was quite another. I feared humiliation, that I couldn't rightly divide God's Word. Comparing myself to the past directors made me uncertain that I could teach the way they did. However, I realized God wasn't asking me to be them. He was asking me to be me and obey Him.

I was also concerned that I couldn't connect with the audience. My first address to the whole camp was scheduled for 45 minutes. As I took the podium, the sweat poured off my face. Fear overwhelmed me. I said everything I'd prepared. To this day, I have no recollection of how or if the audience even responded to what I said. I made my way off the stage. The executive director blinked at me in wide-eyed disbelief and whispered, "Are you finished?"

I whispered back, "Yes! I have nothing else to say."

What I had thought was 45 minutes, was only 15 minutes!

I was never taught how to speak or teach. Still, this was a huge fail. As the weeks went by and I gave the same message to a new group of campers every week, I began to insert examples, stories, and props. By the end of summer, I found confidence and even enjoyment in speaking to an audience. Again, the Lord was developing in me a skill I would need in the future.

I served fourteen years at Kids Across America, with nine of those years as director of KAA-I for nine- through eleven-year-old girls. Starting in 1994, Harold Nash, director of STEP ministry in North Little Rock, AR, brought kids to KAA every summer. Bruce Morgan and Harold had a conversation about me and together they offered me a partnership. KAA only needed me in the summer and STEP needed a girls' director during the school year, so they both hired me, with the understanding that one day I'd pick one job or the other full time. Just as I saw the hand of God moving on my behalf with AIA and KAA, it was again visible in the transition from KAA to STEP Ministries.

CHAPTER 10

STEP, INC.

OPERATION CRACKED HEART

"In 1993, Little Rock's murder rate per capita surpassed that of New York and Los Angeles." An HBO documentary called "Gang Wars: Bangin' in Little Rock" exposed the terrible far-reaching extent of gang activity in the Little Rock and North Little Rock areas of Arkansas. I saw that documentary and heard of a housing project in North Little Rock called Eastgate. STEP Ministry was housed in the Eastgate project, and that's where I was being interviewed to work.

STEP, Serving To Equip People, was a mentoring inner city ministry that began in 1986 when gang activity was strong. Local churches, The Bible Church of Little Rock, Fellowship Bible Church, and Cornerstone Bible Fellowship, were convicted to address this problem, and STEP was born. The logical place to begin was with the children of Eastgate. I met some STEP kids at KAA when they attended camp, and they came into my world. If I worked for STEP, I would be going into their world. STEP's strategy was to intervene in the kids' lives before the gangs did which gave them a hope for a different life.

I also learned there had been a huge drug bust in Eastgate that February right before Valentine's Day called "Operation Cracked Heart." This story was on the evening news all over Arkansas. A lot of drug dealers were taken out of Eastgate. This caused my friends deep concern when I told them I had just been hired to work at STEP, and while I understood their reservations. I was confident of the Lord's leading, so I responded to the call of God to join STEP Ministry in 1995, serving as the Girls' Ministry Director.

A DIFFERENT POVERTY

Although I wasn't raised in wealth, we always had enough. STEP showed me a different poverty. The kids in the housing project were mostly raised by single moms. Any men in the neighborhood were there illegally, staying with the women. I saw welfare becoming a way of life, rather than a steppingstone to independence. Rent, food, and medical care were all provided by well-meaning government programs, but we saw the destructive dependence it created, which became an attitude of entitlement. Adults and children alike thought they were owed these things that the rest of America had to purchase. Many times, money was spent for fun and entertainment before bills were paid. I was face-to-face with a different culture, with a different set of rules.

At first, I thought the Eastgate kids didn't live by any rules. However, as I grew to know them, I realized they were following a set of rules; they just weren't my set of rules. Ruby K. Payne's book, *A Framework for Understanding Poverty*, had become a manual for the training STEP gave the mentors. Payne outlines the rules of poverty, middle class, and wealth. They are all lifestyle actions and predictors, but they differ from each other. For those in poverty, money is to be spent, education is an abstract, not a reality. In general, their driving force is relationships, and entertainment dulls pain. For the middle class, money is to be saved, education is crucial for success, and their driving force is work and achievement. For the wealthy, money is to be invested, education is necessary for tradition and maintaining social and political connections, and their driving force is financial, political and social connections. Rather than making incorrect assumptions about the kids, we needed to understand their set of rules and adjust our prejudgements.

MENTORING MENTORS

"Write out all the expectations you have about this mentoring experience. What do you expect to accomplish?" I was training mentors with a visual exercise.

After everyone finished, I said, "Ball up that sheet of paper and throw it into the trash."

Mentors needed to grasp that their understandings should be left behind. Unmet expectations and agendas could leave a mentor disappointed and disillusioned. If they approached the experience with no preconceived ideas, God could guide the relationship and the mentor's own trust in the Lord would grow. Their only job was to love their assigned kid, warts and all. The mentors began to understand that the kids were taught different values, and those values weren't wrong, just different.

Personally, I knew that without key people in my life, my mentors, my basketball talent would never have developed. I was the beneficiary of mentoring input from several teachers and coaches, so I knew firsthand what a difference just one person can make in the life of another. Mentoring had been my experience and success, so now I was able to train others to be that important person for inner city girls. I had been given much, so now it was my time to pass it on.

> **"...from everyone who has been given much, much will be demanded; and from the one who has been entrusted with much, much more will be asked." Luke 12:48b**

A quiet and unintentional relationship also grew between the STEP mentors and me. When these women heard my lessons for the girls, they began to trust me to give them God's wisdom. Several came to me privately and shared issues in their own lives. The Lord used me as His message-bearer to bring truth into real-life situations. Several of these precious women who came out to be mentors, also became my dear friends. Within our relationship a give-and-take developed, and the mentoring went both ways. They learned from me and I learned from them.

A current mentor who followed me through several ministries said, "Alexis is a mentor of mentors, and makes us feel safe and secure. She draws boundaries around us and releases us from taking on responsibilities that are not ours. Her extreme support keeps us going in the right direction. We always know what is coming because she communicates with us. We feel loved and valued, so we can make the girls we mentor feel that, too."

BUILDING TRUST

Diana stood with the group, proudly smiling, waiting for the camera to click.

I looked at her and thoughtlessly said, "What's wrong with your hair? You know you need to fix it."

The room became silent. Diana's face was downcast. The other kids' quietness made me realize I had overstepped. I thought I was helping, but they didn't agree. I hurt Diana's feelings and offended the entire group. Unless I did something quickly, it could be the beginning of distrust and defensiveness. Realizing that I should think about the perception before I spoke was a lesson I had to learn several times. To fix the awkward moment, I apologized to her and the whole group. Because the group saw my apology, they began to trust my integrity.

Working with inner city kids at KAA, where they were out of their element, didn't prepare me for entering their world at STEP. At camp, the leaders were like stars and deserved to be respected. When I walked into the world of Eastgate Terrace Housing Project, entering the kids' world, I was no longer a star. Initially I wasn't trusted. It had to be earned. I realized I was on trial. I was new to their world, and they were suspicious. As time went on and they became more comfortable with me, I earned their trust and watched their guard drop. I even saw them become protective when there were possible threats to me.

When I became acquainted with the girls, we found common ground. Some wanted to be the center of attention and were outrageously loud and animated. I could identify with that. Some saw no purpose to studying subjects in school because the classes meant nothing to them. I could identify with that, too. For a few, basketball was the center of their world, and everything else was secondary. I could identify with that!

I began to realize God had prepared me with a message for these girls. As I directed teaching times for the girls and their mentors, I spoke from my own experiences. The difficult things in my life became stories I could share, springboards for truth. This is still the case today. When God teaches me something, I feel obligated to share it with others so they can learn too.

STEP staff, mentors, families and I rejoiced when one of our kids finished high school, entered or graduated from college, walked down an aisle to be married, got and held a job. All of these achievements were visible proofs some of our kids had taken responsibility for their lives. The rejoicing in my heart when one of our kids did the right thing was deep and solid.

Sometimes our kids turned the wrong way, the way of pregnancy, the way of crime, the way of dropping out of school. Sadness and heartbreak filled my heart when one chose a destructive way. I knew the continued devastation that stood before them. Even though I wanted desperately to "fix it," I knew only God could do that. It was just my place to love them.

Always, the door was open for them to return and many did. Interestingly, when they made destructive choices, usually they stopped coming around STEP. When they turned back to right thinking, they would come around again. And I was there to welcome the prodigals back home. It went something like this:

"Hi, Miss Alexis!"

"Well, look who's here!"

"I'm sorry. I've been doing bad things."

"I know."

"How'd you know?"

"You stopped coming around. That always tells us you were up to something wrong. But we're so glad you're back!"

We taught them values from the Bible, which they discussed with their mentors. When they embraced and began to own these values, we saw success. For example, one year we were teaching the kids about how to handle conflict. There were three possible responses: Attack, work it out, or escape.

One day, I overheard a girl verbally attacking another in the next room. When the attacked girl was asked what she would do about it, she thought a minute and said, "I think I'll just overlook it."

These godly changes of direction brought tears to our eyes. The kids were choosing godly behavior over their old norm. There was no diploma for being kind, selfless and self-controlled, but in God's kingdom, these are valuable.

"WE GOT YOUR BACK!"

As I was backing out of the parking lot, a car hit my rear bumper. The driver jumped out of her car, screaming, "I'll get paid. I'm getting a new car!"

Shaking, I got out of my car and saw she had a baby in her back seat.

"Is the baby all right? Is he all right?"

"The baby's all right!" she said. "I'm getting a new car!"

The commotion brought several of the Eastgate moms out of their apartments. They hurried over to the parking lot and stood with me. After working at STEP for several years, I developed relationships with the moms of our girls.

They asked me with great respect, "What happened Ms. Alexis? Are you all right?"

When the moms heard the other driver and saw her actions, they said, "Ms. Alexis, we got your back!"

I was grateful to have their visible support and humbled that they'd stand with me. Their presence brought me a sense of calm. God had begun a great work in that neighborhood, and I was part of it. How grateful I was. End of story: the other driver and I both got a ticket—and nobody got a new car.

DO WHAT YOU HAVE TO DO

A girl I'll call Cassandra came into STEP when she was twelve. She was being raised in a little shack full of boxes and cockroaches right across the road from Eastgate. Her loving grandmother was old, but protective. When we asked permission for her to take part in STEP Ministry, her grandmother said we would have to come get her and bring her home every time. We gladly agreed. She had a younger brother and sister for whom she accepted the heavy burden of responsibility because her grandmother was frail. She slept with her siblings on a mattress on the floor, got them up in the mornings, fed them and readied them for school. Although everything surrounding her was uncertain and hopeless, she rose to do whatever the situation required.

When we remarked about how mature and responsible she was, Cassandra said, “You just do what you have to do.”

That phrase seemed to come to her again and again, as her life moved ahead. During the early years, she and I spent time together sharing our lives on a deep level and growing in the Lord. She began to see a difference between “doing what she had to do” and being confident. Together, we sought God’s choices for her which built her into the confident young lady she is today.

One day a group of volunteers fixed up a rent house for their little family, and she finally had a real bed and a room of her own in which to spend her senior year. During these years, she embraced a godly life style. The choices she made were wrapped tightly with her desire to please God.

After high school, Cassandra moved on to college with help from her STEP mentor. She spent time in the military, being deployed overseas, doing what she had to do. She met her future husband, married, and gave birth to a boy first, then a girl. Her husband brought two other children into the marriage, so she was now raising four children. She was doing what she had to do. During this time, she slowly worked on and completed her college degree. Doing what she had to do.

Always, this godly woman sought wisdom, seeking steps toward her future, and never leaning on her hard beginnings. She was the poster child for C. S. Lewis’ quote, “You can’t go back and change the beginning, but you can start where you are and change the ending.”

Everyone loved her and followed her lead. She followed me closely and always put herself near me. Her life was one of putting one foot in front of the other, secure in her relationship with Christ. Understanding each step was an opportunity that could lead to another opportunity has allowed her to walk victoriously through some rough situations. Cassandra has accomplished more than most people, "doing what she had to do."

BEATING THE ODDS

Daron, a young man being raised in a two-bedroom apartment in Eastgate also joined STEP. Although there were six people in that apartment, they rarely spoke, so things were quiet. Of his 15 cousins, he was the only one not in Resource Classes at school. He was paired up with a young mentor who had a college degree and high hopes for him. They met faithfully for years. Later he confided that he was just waiting for the mentor to NOT show up. But that mentor remained faithful to the Lord and to him. This young man was understanding what faithfulness looked like. When he was invited to his mentor's home for a meal, he was surprised that people actually sat around a table and had a conversation while they ate.

One Christmas, the mentor gifted him a few things that were badly needed and told him he loved him. Later when telling this story as an adult, tears rolled down Daron's face as he shared, "I was fourteen years old, and no one had ever told me they loved me!"

This relationship grew stronger and closer. During these years, he spent hours at the STEP building and came to my office often. This was an informal involvement, but I got to see his growth and maturity happen right before my eyes as person after person poured into his life. In his junior year, his mom lost her job, then her home. All her children were just told to find some place to live. They had to find a relative and ask if they could stay. By the time he was a senior, he was truly homeless, so his STEP mentor invited him to live in his apartment. His senior year came and went, and he graduated. He continued to enjoy his mentor and his mentor's parents, working at STEP

Ministry for a time, but he was just floating along. He had no sense of direction, no initiative and no vision. He wasn't sure who he was or how to live.

During these years, the Lord was building something magnificent within him. He learned how to live a godly life and his driving force became a devotion to the Lord. The reality of this godly life became visible through his mentor. A few people began to paint a picture of his potential future, which included college. However, he already had an idea about that. Daron had never thought about going to college because only special people went to college, and he wasn't special. Finally, one of those visions began to take hold in his mind. He decided to try it. And try it he did! Today, he holds two master's degrees, an M.B.A. and Master of Arts in Human Resource Management.

During all this education, he married and became a father—in that order, something rare for Eastgate kids. When he stepped into the role of a father, he leaned heavily on the men in his life who had mentored him. Because he was now educated and earning a living, he became a financial resource for his family. For people living in poverty, when one earns a paycheck, everyone thinks it's for everybody.

At one point, he even said, "My family thinks I am the bank."

After his daughter's birth, however, Daron realized he had to set some financial boundaries for his family.

Today he desires to be a godly example for his relatives and their children. He wants to build a vision for them to understand what he came to slowly understand: that they can go to college, can get an education, can hold down a regular job, and can pay their own way in the world. He wants to be known as a cycle-breaker. He wants his extended family to know they can do this, too, and there are no limits and no caps. Although this young man has achieved the American dream, his walk with the Lord is most important. Today he has a job with a communications company where he oversees 170 people in the United States and beyond. He definitely beat the odds.

Society would have looked at Daron and never expected much from him. Because I was also one who wasn't expected to succeed, I identified with him. I watched him transform in developing a close relationship with God and with godly mentors. He was well-respected amongst the mentors and the kids as a young man of character.

CHAPTER 11

ABSTINENCE

NOT ALL GOOD

"Who wants to marry a virgin?" Harold Nash asked a classroom of high school students. Most of the boys' hands went up.

Also sitting in that room was a stunned young lady. She was watching her boyfriend admit he wanted to marry a virgin, yet was pressuring her to have sex with him every time they went out. After that class, she broke up with him.

Although STEP experienced blessings and growth in many of the kids, it wasn't all positive. One main frustration was the contrast between God's word and the world in which the kids lived. We often taught a lesson at STEP, knowing some children would walk into a home where the opposite was being lived out before them. For instance, we taught that sex before marriage was wrong, but they went home to their mom living with a man.

Yet the Bible says:

> **"Marriage should be honored by all, and the marriage bed kept pure, for God will judge the adulterer and all the sexually immoral." Hebrews 13:4**

Some Eastgate kids lived in homes where there was structure, morality, and love. However, illicit sex was rampant amongst many of the residents. The norm being lived out in front of them was short-term non-marital relationships, often times resulting in pregnancy. Then the fathers disappeared, leaving their children behind. Because my father had disappeared, I could also identify with that.

I still don't know why my parents divorced when I was seven years old. I only understood a little of why my mother couldn't stay married to my father. And yet, I hurt over all I lost, all I hadn't known, and all I didn't have because of those years of not knowing and not being with my father. My head understood but my heart didn't.

c. 1971. Four-year-old Alexis with her biological father.

He remarried, created another family and I saw little of him the remainder of my growing-up years. The man who had once held me in his arms and brought joy to my little girl heart now held other people in a family circle that didn't include me. Because I had no contact with my biological father through the years, he became to me a little more than a distant, vaguely familiar relative. Instead, my stepfather, Pops, was my dad.

God had uniquely prepared me for this work. Abstinence and my relationship with the Lord were the strong messages I shared with them. My personal commitment to purity, based on my relationship with the Lord, was stated at every turn. I was the walking model of making a different choice. The students needed to make their own choices, but now they knew it was a choice. They could choose a different way.

RESPECT

After standing in chaos, I caught the eye of a male student. I threw my basketball at him, and he caught it. He threw it back. I saw another student looking at me and threw it again. He returned it. Two more throws and returns brought the boisterous room to complete silence. The students looked at me with curiosity. Finally the room became quiet, and I could start.

I was invited to speak on abstinence at a small high school in the Arkansas Delta. When I entered this poor school, I noticed the windows were covered with sheets. I became nervous. I was led to the library where the students were gathered. The teachers left me there with over fifty disorderly, out-of-control students. Looking around, I saw there was no introduction or support. Everything was out of order, and the students had no intention of quieting or listening. I rehearsed a lot of insecure thoughts. What if they don't listen to me? What if they laugh at me? What if they don't believe what I have to say? Fear overwhelmed me. That's when I threw the ball.

The students' curiosity quieted them, and my fears dissolved. I began by sharing my college basketball experiences. They listened. As the abstinence message followed, they listened even more intently. Many students expressed shock and disbelief at abstaining from sex until marriage.

After that response, I boldly asked, "Why are you shocked?"

Now, I was free to share the entire message with confidence.

Because I was an adult who was a virgin, waiting for the right man, I told the boys, "It is important for you to respect girls. Pay attention to how you treat them."

A seemingly popular young man raised his hand and said, "I've had sex with half the girls in this room! And you're telling us to respect them when they don't respect themselves!"

Taken back, I turned toward the girls and demanded, "Did you hear that girls? If what he's saying is true, you need to learn how to respect yourself if you expect anyone else to respect you. And young men, there is no excuse to treat the girls like that. Boys, would you want someone treating your sister like that? Girls, would you want someone treating your brother like that?"

Everyone responded with a resounding, "No!"

"Why?"

"Because it's disrespectful." The dialogue that followed showed the students began to grasp what respect should look like.

I affirmed they were precious, valuable, and worthy. They heard what I said and respected it. The students who heard the message of abstinence revealed they understood premarital sex was an option, not a rite of passage, not an expectation, not a given. An option. They had the power to make a choice, and "No" was just as possible as "Yes."

When the teachers in the hall heard me finish, they rejoined the class. They didn't understand why the students were so quiet.

A NEW START

At another high school where I gave my abstinence presentation, a female student began weeping, tears flowing and couldn't be comforted. Something I said had upset her, but I needed to continue with the message. A STEP staff member went to visit with her. When she could finally speak, she shared that she tried to do what I did, maintain virginity until marriage. She resisted the temptation to have unmarried sex, but she had finally given in, and now she couldn't forgive herself. She was devastated and full of sorrow. The staff member spoke to her about "secondary virginity." That means if you've already had sex, you can choose to never have it again until you marry. This precious girl needed to forgive herself, turn the page and start over with a clear resolve to keep that boundary. She left with hope in her heart.

CHAPTER 12

WELFARE TO WORK

A NEW BEGINNING

"I'm here to inquire about the opening. Could you please share with me what is involved?"

I was investigating the position of Director of the Care Center, connected to the Church at Rock Creek, which served adult clientele who needed assistance.

After working at STEP for eleven years, I built some intense relationships with true friends who became my family. I sensed an unrest I couldn't explain. Although I loved what I was doing, I was becoming burned out. It seemed every waking thought I had, every book I read, every activity I did revolved around STEP. There was no balance to my life. I couldn't identify what troubled me. The Lord was leading me to something new, but what?

During this turbulent time, I crossed paths with a longtime friend who gave me a lead on a job. A local church was searching for a director of their Care Center. I applied, but this was the first time I ever applied for a job where I knew no one. I needed a change, but the hiring process seemed uncertain.

Before going to an appointment, I wrote three things in my journal to affirm for me this job was of God and for me. The criteria included the amount of the salary, the start date, and whether there was a prerequisite of church membership.

The pastor, Mark Evans replied excitedly, "Great! We need someone to oversee the Care Center, which includes a food bank, computer classes, and conducting job and life skill workshops. Until now, all these positions have been manned by volunteers, but it's getting so large, we need a director to coordinate everything."

As the dialogue continued, and I learned more detailed expectations for the position, I wondered if I could do any of it. I was to oversee programs already in place, rather than create something brand new. "I've done none of these things before," I said.

"Don't worry," he said. "We'll guide you the whole way."

As the conversation progressed, I had forgotten the three criteria I had written down.

Thinking I gathered all the information I needed, I picked up my purse to leave.

He said, "Oh, let me tell you this: the salary is (just what I had set as the salary! Exactly!), the start date is whenever you can finish up with your other job, and you don't have to be a member of this church to have this position."

I was stunned.

My shocked expression caused him to say, "Is that enough? Is that all right?"

He didn't know he just answered all three criteria.

Finally, it occurred to me that this wasn't just an informational meeting, but an interview! I asked, "Well, I guess I'm hired?"

He smiled and said, "Yes."

Leading me away from his office, to the building I would oversee, I was surprised, taken aback. My office would be huge!

The floors were stained concrete. Furniture was new and current. Best of all, volunteers were already in place.

Walking away from STEP meant I was also leaving my support base. God was using my inner turbulence to move me in a new direction. I cried when I shared with the kids and mentors I was leaving. I had such a deep love for them, but my turmoil was undeniable.

A young girl in the program said with tears streaming down her face, "If I were in your shoes, I'd be obedient to God too."

She understood my tears and reminded me I was moving from STEP out of obedience. After watching me work for years, she understood my life belongs to Christ. This made my departure less painful. I never wanted the kids or the mentors to think I was abandoning them. I hoped they understood the gospel and how much God loves them. My prayer was that they would live a life devoted to God. Those mentors and those children will be forever etched in my heart. This season of serving the Lord was ending, and I was looking forward to the next step.

During this time of uncertainty and change, I journaled my feelings about what God was showing me. One day as I journaled, God brought to my attention I had made some "friends" who were taking me away from my close walk with Him, hindering what God was calling me to do. As I wrote, the Lord told me I couldn't take those long-time "friends" with me to my next step. I needed to leave them behind.

Leaving familiar emotions and responses behind was terrifying because I knew I would have to replace them with new responses.

After wrestling with this and seeking direction, God eventually showed the names of my "friends:" anxiety, unforgiveness, selfishness, and insecurity.

Naming them helped relieve my stress. This was followed by overwhelming sorrow because I disappointed God. I realized through the years I embraced those negative emotions, and they began to influence my thinking. I couldn't take these things into my next assignment.

As I continued to write, God gave me peace, forgiveness, selflessness, and security, my new "friends." The Lord shifted my paradigm. A new peace overwhelmed me as my thinking cleared. I determined to forgive everyone I needed to forgive, understand that all I do is not about me, and find complete security in Christ. The relief of this new perception made me feel like a brand-new person.

CARE CENTER

Nervous excitement filled me on day one at the Care Center because I knew no one. I was scared and anxious, but as I entered the building, my new assistant and a group of volunteers embraced me warmly. Everyone was welcoming and loving. I shadowed a few of the staff members who served in the various programs and learned how things worked. The ministries included the Food Bank program (giving food to people in the community who need it), Job & Life Skill Workshops (preparing people to enter the job market) and the Computer Lab (teaching basic computer skills).

As programs flowed, I saw new ideas I could add (such as a GED program) without moving the things that already worked. The volunteers and I warmed up to each other and they grew to trust me. I encouraged them and praised their efforts. The teams for the three ministries began to form as I found my place in the program. More and more people came out to serve in the Care Center.

The workshops taught skills that linked to careers. Most of our clientele were welfare recipients. Arkansas Department of Health Services (DHS) required them to attend this mandatory workshop in order to keep their benefits and train to enter the job market. Each six-week adult workshop went from Tuesday–Friday, 9 a.m.-3 p.m.

Through these workshops, I was speaking daily with our students, as well as organizing guest speakers and field trips. Our classroom was large, and the tables were set up in a U shape. This made it easy to see every student's face as we presented new ideas to them. Speakers taught such things as how to write a resume, how to dress appropriately, how to be interviewed, how to talk on the phone, how to budget, how to have good hygiene and how to do housekeeping. Many didn't hold a job because they couldn't manage conflict, so we addressed that, as well. All the time, I was sharing the love of God, His Word, and applying it to specific situations.

MODEL OF FORGIVENESS

My mom was born into this world unwanted.

I'm constantly amazed at how my own life experiences prepared me to do the work God set before me. At the Care Center, I found the ability to forgive was an important skill. I learned forgiveness from my parents.

My mom's birth mother literally handed her over to a childless couple when she was ten days old. She simply wrote out a statement she was giving her baby to the couple. No legal guardianship papers were signed, and that was that. My mother's new parents were elated and grateful. Because the new baby girl was their only child, she became the center of their world. Home was a place of structure, rules and love. Although she sometimes wondered why her birth mother had made this decision and sometimes felt rejected because of it, she didn't dwell there. She knew she was loved and treasured. Her parents taught her what it meant to love people. Because of that, my mom knew she wanted to forgive her biological mother even though she didn't understand everything.

One day during her childhood, a cousin showed Mom a picture of her birth mother. As she burned that photo into her brain, unanswered questions bounced around in her mind. Here was a stranger who looked a lot like her. She wondered how else they might be alike.

On a warm beautiful day, Mom, then 20 years old, attended her great grandmother's funeral. It was there she first saw her birth mother in person, recognizing her from the picture. She stole looks at her mother all through the service, imprinting the image into her mind. However, because the same cousin said her birth mother still wanted nothing to do with her, neither spoke to the other. That chapter has stayed closed to this day.

Mom's adoptive mother passed away when she was eight. Her dad did lawn work for a lawyer, so he asked for some advice. Her dad explained that my mom's birth mother had just signed over her parental rights in a handwritten note, giving the baby to them. The lawyer recommended he legally adopt my mom. At the age of fourteen, she was legally adopted by her father in the state of Texas.

Mom decided that she would forgive her birth mother because she couldn't hate her. The decision to relinquish her daughter had been between her and God. When those thoughts of rejection interrupted her thinking, she dismissed them and chose not to linger there. I admired my mother's decision to choose forgiveness rather than bitterness. Because of that choice, she was a better role model for me by passing the baton of forgiveness with a firm and sure hand. I accepted that baton, not realizing I needed to forgive unanswered questions in my future, too.

FORGIVENESS AND FREEDOM

Always, there was an emptiness in my heart associated with my family situation. When Pops married Mom, he became my true dad. He and I had a close relationship, so my heart had no void for a dad.

Never could I come to a place of rest on the issue of my biological father. He had left us. He had never maintained a relationship with me. Somehow, I was cheated out of something only he could provide. There was no resting place for me within these thoughts.

On a long drive to Victoria from Little Rock, a strange thought interrupted my thinking. Out of the blue, came "visit the sick." The Holy Spirit reminded me God is pleased when we visit the sick. My biological father was in a nursing home and sick. This could be the reason for me to visit him. Linking both thoughts brought me to a place of understanding I was holding him hostage with these thoughts. Deliberately, I decided to let him off the hook.

I went to visit him in the nursing home even before going to Mom's. I walked peacefully into the room and saw a very sick, weak old man. Compassion filled my heart, and the next few hours were filled with easy conversation and laughter. At the end of that visit, I sensed a release, a freedom. I was no longer bound to an idea of irretrievable loss, but rather of moving forward in peace.

Nine months later when my mom called to tell me that he had died, I was instantly aware of a few things. I had already chosen to forgive him, so I was no longer burdened with that. I didn't have the emotional connections to him that a daughter would normally have for her father, but I also knew I needed to attend his funeral out of respect for the fact he was my biological father. Finally, I knew I needed to be there to support my siblings who had known him longer.

Holding onto the pain of my father's abandonment could've caused me to seek out male attention, any kind of male attention. That would have caused certain destruction down the road. Refusing to forgive my father might have soured me on the whole male species, leading me to not trust any man, which is a different kind of destruction. Moreover, laying all the blame on my mom could have forever created a chasm between us. There was nothing good down the road of unforgiveness. Choosing to forgive my parents released me from the bondage of these wrong responses. Mom and I have a close relationship, I don't hold all guys to blame, and my choices have left me untarnished by sexual destruction. These lessons in forgiveness helped me empathize with the students at the Care Center.

JOB AND LIFE SKILL WORKSHOPS

"Make sure to sign in everyday so I can turn the attendance sheet in to DHS," I said. "Never forget that everything I do is to teach you about how to build a strong work ethic. And you must sign out at the end of the day, just like you would at a job."

For the first few weeks, I reminded the students of the importance of signing in when they arrived. One morning I stopped reminding them. The next day, several signed in, but others didn't. As the meeting started, I called the names of those who signed in to come forward. When they got to the front, I showed them a jewelry box with lots of jewelry in it. They were invited to take one piece home with them to keep. The ones still sitting asked why they couldn't do that, too.

I told them, "You aren't even at work. You didn't sign in."

Suddenly one exasperated student stood up, gathered her personal items and was preparing to walk out the door. Her body language expressed anger and frustration.

I called out to her. She diverted her eyes, held up her hand and growled, "Don't talk to me!"

I went back to helping the other students pick out their jewelry. Soon I heard her call out, "Ms. Alexis."

I raised my hand in the same manner she had and said, "Don't talk to me!"

She threw her backpack over her shoulder and stomped out. I went on with my day and explained to the class the importance of doing exactly what was required, even if it appears small, inconvenient and unnecessary. We discussed the concept of integrity and how important it is to do the right thing even when no one's looking.

The next day the angry lady returned and said awkwardly, "Ms. Alexis, I owe you an apology. I told my mom what I did, and she said I shouldn't treat that nice lady like that. I'm sorry for the way I acted."

I laughed and told her I wasn't mad at her, but also that I told a lot of people about how she acted.

I wanted others to hear her story and understand accountability and integrity are important but throwing a fit won't ever get you what you want. We both laughed and were on good terms. Hopefully, that little lesson will never leave the class, and they learned every rule is important. When someone in authority asks you to do something, it's right to submit.

BAGGAGE

Another student came to class undeniably downcast and suspicious, shoulders slumped. She wouldn't talk at all, but she attended faithfully every day. Class members tried reaching out to include her, but she rejected their efforts. She was imprisoned in insecurity. However, as the weeks progressed and her trust in her classmates grew, she started to speak about her issues. Because she experienced mental, emotional and physical abuse at the hands of her husband, she was broken and fragile. Her damaged self-image told her she had no worth. On the other hand, she heard speakers pour words of life into her every week. She listened as the speakers respected and affirmed the class as people of worth and significance. She began to believe what she heard.

Most of the students came into class with baggage from a life of making poor choices. That meant many came in defeated, feeling worthless. We—the speakers and myself—intentionally spoke words of life into their lives. Often, it took the whole six weeks to build up someone, helping them understand they had significance in the world.

One day, I invited three professional counselors to form a panel discussion in front of the class. To start, I asked questions about how to handle anger. As the therapists spoke, Ann burst out crying. She spewed out all the brutalities that her husband had been doing to her. He hit her regularly, beat her down emotionally by criticizing her body, degrading her at every turn. She was indeed scarred. At this point, she'd left him physically, but he was still emailing her with threats. She was still in bondage mentally. Everyone in the class demanded she leave him, stay away from him and block his emails. They were almost angry with her. Although the class could see clearly what she should do, the therapists explained the terrible bond that causes women to return to such a situation. Understanding the hold an abuser can have on a person opened the door for the entire class to share where they were as well.

Everyone had issues. The room was filled with vulnerability, transparency and eventually hope. This young lady needed healing from the abuse heaped on her and the lies she believed. She left the class affirmed and encouraged. Every time she came to class, we saw the incredible change in her. She was becoming empowered by the truths she was embracing. On graduation day, she held her head high.

Eleven years later, she still works at the same company and has been promoted several times.

GOOD OR BAD

"Well, I have some good news and some bad news. Which one do you want first?"

The financial component of the Job and Life Skill classes convicted me my own personal finances were not in order. I spoke to a volunteer who had become a friend. She was good with numbers and budgets, and she agreed to help me. I was ashamed to show her my numbers. I realized that I had dug a debt hole and couldn't get out. I was teaching others how to stick to a budget but couldn't do it myself. My main concern was her view of me. She was a volunteer in my program, I was the director, but still I knew I needed to ask for help. She looked at the amount of money the church paid me, and the amount of my bills, including a credit card debt.

"The bad news," I replied.

I expected her to tell me to sell my house, and I was willing to do that.

Instead, she said, "The bad news is you don't make enough money to pay your bills, let alone your debt!"

I knew that, which was why I asked for her help. Then I asked her for the good news.

She said, "I'm going to write you a check to pay off your debt—all of it!"

I refused, acknowledging I'd made the debt, and I should fix it.

Her response humbled me. "My husband and I have been blessed financially, and we want to do this. We can't do what you do. Please let us do this for you!"

I was stunned and embarrassed. I wanted to cry. But I was so incredibly grateful. Peace overwhelmed me as I humbly accepted her generous gift. Glory to God!

PREGNANT?

"Any chance you might be pregnant?" asked the clerk at the ER.

That day I woke up with my head spinning so badly I could hardly stand up. When I called my friend to take me to the ER, she agreed and came quickly.

Now, as a speaker for abstinence, I was a little insulted by the question. I whispered, "No!"

Finally, I was admitted to the ER, where a nurse took my vitals and asked about my symptoms. She also asked, "Any chance you might be pregnant?"

I guess the hospital people didn't talk to each other. Again, I quietly said, "No."

Someone else came into my cubicle to check my blood pressure. Again, the question was asked, "Any chance you might be pregnant?"

I was getting angry and offended. "No, I'm not pregnant!" I rolled my eyes to my friend, and she just smiled.

A doctor entered the room, assessed my condition and ordered an CT Scan. Before leaving, he asked, "Any chance you might be pregnant?"

I said in a too loud voice, "Absolutely NOT!"

The orderly came for me and wheeled me to the exam room. As I lay there, the technician bent down and whispered in my ear, "Any chance you might be pregnant?"

I was so annoyed, I shouted, "No. I'm a 39-year-old virgin!"

The tech asked me with great excitement, "Have you seen the movie, 'The 40-Year-Old Virgin?'"

"This isn't a movie," I said. "This is the real deal."

He left the room in a rush. Soon people walked by the window and peeked in. I guess a 39-year-old virgin was a curiosity they needed to see for themselves.

This turned out to be one of my students' favorite stories! Because of that, I had confidence in continuing to share my purity message. Seeing my words impact adults affirmed and encouraged me to stay on this path. I was a living breathing example of abstinence until marriage. Because of this story, some students said they would start practicing abstinence, too. They could see the freedom I had and could choose it for themselves.

LESSONS LEARNED

"We're going shopping at Goodwill, and we'll have a contest," I told the students. "See who can buy the most items for $25. You can keep what you buy."

Excited students lined up for their money. Many of these adult students hadn't bought clothing in a long time because their children's needs came first. Some didn't even know their own sizes.

The purpose of that trip was to show the students they could stretch what little they had and make it work. One lady was put off by the idea of going to Goodwill to shop. She had too much pride to go there.

Several of the students had larger cars, so we just filled all the cars and drove together. When we arrived at Goodwill, the students went all directions. A few paired up to help each other because they hadn't shopped for themselves in a long time. Miss Prideful stayed with me, still refusing to shop. As some students came to me, proud of their bargains, her pride began to evaporate. Little by little, she too, got excited.

Finally, she quietly told me, "Maybe I'll shop too."

After shopping, we ate at a nice restaurant where they ordered from a menu and had food requiring a fork. This was another life skill. It was gratifying to see how comfortable the students had become in that social setting.

The class had become a wonderful group of friends. It had taken weeks to build them up so they believed in their significance in the world. All the speakers and activities had instilled worth. The students finally understood they didn't have to be condemned by their past or their own bad choices.

IMMEDIATE DISMISSAL

A pregnant student stomped into my office, disgusted and angry. "I'm pregnant," she said, "and they were smoking weed in the car!"

The top rule at the workshop was drugs of any kind wouldn't be tolerated and were cause for immediate dismissal. Accusations weren't allowed, and I wasn't sure who had smoked the weed. I knew who she traveled with, so I just invited one of the guys to come to my office.

He softly and fearfully walked up to my doorway.

Dramatically, I held my head in my hands and with a firm voice I said, "I'm so disappointed. I don't know what to do!"

He immediately said, "Well, I wasn't the only one smoking weed."

He admitted he did it without being asked.

The other young man stood in the hallway watching us, secretly motioning to him not to confess. Too little, too late.

I walked to the hall and addressed him. "Do you remember the rules we had at the beginning?"

"Yes."

"Well the rule says any drug use is cause for immediate dismissal. I guess you made your choice. You're dismissed. You won't graduate."

Shocked he said, "I can't believe you're putting me out."

"I'm not putting you out," I said. "You put your own self out. I'm so disappointed you would do this."

He argued, "But it's the last day!"

"It doesn't matter what day it is," I said. "You knew the consequence."

Head lowered, he walked miserably down the hall. Still standing in my doorway, I turned to the one still in my office and said, "You're dismissed, too!"

His face crumpled, and he began to cry and said, "Ms. Alexis, please tell my mom."

I told him, "You're a grown man. Tell her yourself."

After my initial shock, I was angry at them for exposing a pregnant woman to marijuana. Those men will never forget this lesson. They'll think twice about taking drugs into the work force.

The whole class couldn't believe I dismissed them both on Friday before the Sunday graduation. Everybody learned rules matter. Consequences are certain. Obedience is required.

GRADUATION

It was graduation day. I woke up with crowded thoughts. My students had become a kind of family that wouldn't exist after today. The security and support they found with each other would be gone. They became my family, too. My heart was filled with both sadness as each person went their separate way and pride at their progress. The growth of confidence in each helped me understand they were walking away with skills and potential for success. My work was done.

My job was to equip adults for the world of employment. When the students completed the six weeks with no more than three absences, they took part in a graduation ceremony held at the church during a regular Sunday service.

I stood on the stage consumed with joy because I knew this was a huge step for the students. Completing the workshop involved sacrifice, and they realized this was an investment in their future. Each student wore a white cap and gown, complete with gold tassels. As each name was read and they stepped toward me to receive their Certificate of Completion, I saw many tears. Because we had worked so closely and I knew them so well, emotion rolled over both of us.

Hundreds of people in the congregation were witnesses to their success. The church members cheered loudly for all the graduates, so those with no family present felt honored too. For some students, this was the first time they'd ever graduated from anything. It was an important moment.

After the ceremony, the students and their families were invited to a banquet at Embassy Suites, where the celebration continued. The excited group became subdued and respectful as they entered the banquet room. White tablecloths and napkins, floral centerpieces, and fine china set the scene for an elegant meal. Waiters and waitresses appeared to serve this precious group. It was imperative they understood they were important, valuable, and significant.

After the meal, I joyfully awarded individual framed Certificates of Character to each student, highlighting character qualities such as loyalty, dependability, leadership, dedication. These would serve as a reminder of what I observed developing in them and to speak into their future.

We offered a time called "Say So" during which students took the microphone and expressed whatever they wanted to say about the classes and what they learned. Many said they could now write a resume, they could succeed, and they might even consider college. We heard story after story of empowerment. A few said this group had become like a family they never had. A few expressed this program had helped their marriages and parenting. Some said they even developed a relationship with the Lord. Family members excitedly shared about the changes they witnessed in their loved ones during the class. This special and fun day gave me a sense of accomplishment and affirmation to continue pouring into the lives of adults.

BROKE AGAIN

January 2010, less than a year after my friend paid off my credit card debt, I found myself in credit card debt again. She was right. I didn't make enough money to pay all my bills. I was so disappointed in myself and felt defeated. This bothered me a lot because I experienced the freedom of having no debt. Here I was again, owing money. I desired to never let money control me. The burden of debt weighed heavily on me, but it also drove me toward taking control of the situation.

Because the Lord was convicting me, I set a goal to get all my finances in order. Dave Ramsey's Financial Peace University seemed a great way for me to do just that. I implemented this financial program near the end of January.

The first thing Ramsey recommended was to save $1000 dollars as an emergency fund. I did that immediately using my tax refund. The next requirement was to pay off my debts using the "snowball effect," which means to pay the smallest one off first. Then double the payments on the next debt, and so on till all debts were paid. The third requirement was to figure out exactly what my bills were and save that amount, enough for 6 months. From January to July of 2010, I earned extra money by teaching private basketball lessons, which allowed me to complete all these requirements. My finances were in order and I was out of debt. The freedom I experienced was great, though I didn't understand why this seemed so urgent.

"let no debt remain outstanding..." Romans 13:8a

IN A BOX

Because I came into the Care Center position from several urban ministries, I brought a deeper knowledge of inner city experiences. When I could see expansions, partnerships and other ideas, sometimes I was the only one who could see it. Somehow God was birthing something in me that was new. I could see possibilities beyond what we were already doing. However, because these current programs were already in place, it was unspoken we would continue with them just the way they were. In some ways I felt limited, like I was working in a box.

Although the Care Center was a huge success, other aspects of this position started to become a burden. I began to feel separated from the leadership and isolated. My other jobs had felt like family, but things were different here. Communication was nonexistent, so misconceptions abounded both ways. This situation caused gradual destruction in my confidence, and I was often unsteady. Emotionally, I began to unravel, as I tried to understand an invisible enemy. I just didn't comprehend the dynamic that was happening. Some mornings, I cried all the way to work.

CHAPTER 13

UNEMPLOYED

BLINDSIDED

Two weeks to decide? I was blindsided. My boss told me that my job requirements had changed. Now I was required to join the church that funded the Care Center or find other work. It was an ultimatum. I reminded him that when I was hired, I was told I didn't need membership to work in the Care Center. It didn't matter. I had two weeks to decide.

During those two weeks, I tried to process the situation. I had never been fired before. After the shock wore off, I realized I was incredibly hurt. It was like an attack on my character.

Shaken, I knew I was standing up for the right thing and I knew God was in this. Joining their church was not an option. The church I had attended for several years was family and I was involved leading Bible studies. I had solid friendships there and had found my niche. My pastor was accessible and committed to teaching the Word with integrity. Leaving my church would mean leaving all of that. Just thinking about it made me sick to my stomach. I didn't need two weeks. The choice was clear.

July 2010, I looked at unemployment for the first time in my life. I had never been faced with this kind of life challenge. Overwhelming, emotional, unsteady, questioning thoughts flooded my brain. Was this in fact God making this move for me?

In my heart I had to acknowledge that I did my best, but that season was over.

As I began a new chapter at home, I wrestled with negative thinking and feelings. On one hand, I wanted the organization to be sorry for losing me. Those negative thoughts didn't last long. I began to understand I had gained a lot from my time at the Care Center.

At God's prompting, I wrote and sent a thank-you email to the church, listing all the wonderful things I had learned about God, about myself, and about precious people who need help. The deep relationships built there had blessed and encouraged me. I was honored and privileged to have the opportunities and experiences, which better prepared me for what came next.

Here's what I wrote:

> July 22, 2010
>
> Winter of 2005, the Lord called me to leave my haven (STEP Ministries) to work here. This was a huge step of faith for me, but I knew it was the right step. I can remember saying during the interview, that I knew nothing about running a food bank, computer lab or job/life skills workshop.
>
> The response was, "Don't worry about it, we will train you."
>
> Here I am five years later, and I've gained more knowledge about coordinating different programs than I ever could have imagined.
>
> I am writing just to let you know how much I appreciated this opportunity. I enjoyed connecting with

the volunteers and the people in the community. They became my family away from home. I am so grateful that I was a part of a program that gave individuals a chance to start over in life. I had the opportunity to watch lives change in front of my eyes. To see people give their hearts to Christ made my heart smile. My experience here gave me such an appreciation that you all believed in giving individuals second chances at life. To this I say, "God bless you for doing this."

I also wanted to let you know that my experience in coordinating the food bank was a hit as well. I was able to interact with individuals who just needed to know that they "matter" to somebody. One of the many things that stood out to me was a client who used to receive food assistance from this program, brought in a $50.00 bill to donate because she was blessed and wanted to give back. This money was like $1,000.00 dollars to her. My heart was humbled that she would even think to do this. She expressed how the people (volunteers) helped her when she was down. Thank you for allowing me to be a part of this experience as well.

There is a lot I have gained from my experience in working here. If I had to pick one thing, it would be that no matter how difficult of a life someone has lived, God can and will use them to do a great work for His Kingdom. God kept me humbled and, in a place, where I needed to trust Him always because of the many challenges I faced in counseling with the clients. A ton of their struggles blew me away. One thing never failed; God's grace was enough. He gave me what I needed at the time I needed it.

So, again thank you for allowing me to be a part of this program in sharing the Lord's work to impact the Kingdom of God.

In Him,
Alexis Ware

After hitting SEND, I experienced boundless freedom about choosing the high road and looking for what was good in this experience leading to the unknown.

My last day was on a Friday, so the next day was Saturday and I wouldn't have been working anyway. But, the following Monday, I woke up and had nowhere to go. I had never NOT had a job. Somehow, I felt I should do something. As I was wondering what to do with myself, friends called. Some wanted to take me to lunch, others wanted to ask how to support me and still others just wanted to make sure I was okay.

These first days at home were confusing and fearful, but I experienced a puzzling peace that passed all my understanding.

"And the peace of God, which transcends all understanding, will guard your hearts and your minds in Christ Jesus." Philippians 4:7

Little by little, God was becoming more and more real as my Jehovah Jireh, one of the Hebrew names that means, "my provider." God had led and prepared me uniquely for the work I had just finished. Therefore, I needed to agree that despite how unjust this seemed, God was still in control. Although everything that loomed large before me appeared insecure, I surprisingly calmed down and rested in God's sovereignty. This is why I call the challenging events that brought me to the next fourteen months, "a promotion." Somehow, I knew I was headed somewhere even better. I just couldn't see it yet. However, before that unknown became known, I still needed to walk through an unnerving time of raw and untested faith. The future months became a time of waiting, trusting, growing, a time of R & R, rest and restoration.

THE STRUGGLE IS REAL, BUT GOD IS GOOD

"Do you want to go on vacation with us?" One of my sisters invited me to join her family on a trip to San Diego, California, in August 2010, right after becoming unemployed.

"I don't have a job! How am I going to go on a vacation? I need to be looking for work," I said frantically. The timing of this seemed wrong. What would my friends think of me taking a vacation when I had such a huge need?

I had never taken a real vacation. Every time I had a break, I used it to return to my family in Texas.

"My family and I will pay all the expenses," she said. "We just want you to come with us."

Because I gained great pleasure in being a giver, I learned that it was difficult to be a receiver. But I humbly jumped at the invitation. We had such a great time and it was a welcome relief from the stress of my unemployed life. For that week I didn't even think about what was happening next. I was learning to live only for the moment. My sister didn't realize how much I needed this time away.

When I returned a week later, I was still face-to-face with the unknown. Since my finances were in order, I didn't feel a financial pinch right away. But money was going out, with nothing coming in, and I experienced financial pressure in a new way. My thoughts were based on fear and pride. I never had to ask anybody for help and didn't want to now.

God gave me a self-imposed structure, so every morning, I got up, dressed for work, made my bed, and headed out to a coffee shop (even though I don't drink coffee) with my laptop. My job was to find a job, so that was what I did.

Walking into the nearest coffee shop, I ordered the cheapest drink on the menu, usually tea. Taking my steaming cup, I slid into any available corner, opened my computer and began the job search. The frustration of looking made me realize how difficult it had been for my students in the Care Center. The more I showed up at this coffee shop, the more familiar I became to the regulars and staff.

When the inevitable question came, "What do you do?"

I was overwhelmed with a sudden shame. "I'm in transition and searching for a job," I said.

I had always been validated by what I did, whether it was through basketball or serving in a ministry. This was a true identity crisis. My faith was being tested. Who was I without a title or position? For the first time I was connected to no organization, no position and no group. There was only God.

I sat amongst the coffee shop customers, searching and praying. The employment search was frustrating. Occasionally I was given an opportunity for an interview. Entering each interview full of hope, I answered questions only to be told that I was over-qualified. Nothing came of it. Everything in me commanded I seek a job, any job.

I used this season to have lengthy quiet times. One battle I waged was to prevent fear from overtaking my thoughts. During this time as I spent extended times in God's word, I relaxed when I read and embraced this verse:

"For the spirit God gave us does not make us timid, but gives us power, love and self-discipline." 2 Timothy 1:7

I came to understand that I needed to quit looking for a job and trust God was preparing something specific for me.

"I'm afraid I'm going to miss what God wants me to do," I shared at a prayer meeting.

A friend told me, "God is more interested in you getting what He has for you, than you not getting it."

I understood my striving was unnecessary and my fear was groundless. My job, my only job, was to trust God had my future worked out. To embrace this required a new level of faith.

The more I read and studied, the more I realized how God's Word encourages us to not be afraid. Interestingly, I learned "Fear not" is found 365 times in the Bible, one for each day of the year. It sounded like every day had cause for fear, but every day the Word tells us not to go there. God is in control even when we can't see it.

A newfound intimacy with God developed as words of encouragement jumped off the pages of my Bible. The Lord let me know He could see me, and He loved me. He was, indeed, El Roi, the Hebrew name that means, "the God who sees!"

I remember telling friends, "If I got any closer to God, I'd be in heaven."

SILENT MENTOR

"You 're about to enter a season of receiving," Jill said. "Because you've been a giver, now you'll reap a harvest."

At that time "harvest" looked like a new job, a solid and regular pay check.

God often sent special people to mentor me, move me further along in my spiritual walk, and mature my thinking. Jill was a special mentor. Her passion for God and for people drew me to her. In a crowded room, she made me feel like I was the only one there, and she was my closest friend. She took me under her wing and spoke words of encouragement and life into me.

Unsure what Jill meant by a time of reaping, I held tight to those words. Whenever I wrestled with negative thoughts, becoming weak and directionless, Jill invited me to come by her house and talk. As she stirred up "the gift of God" which was in me, I became reempowered, realigned and ready to move forward.

As the days of unemployment stretched out to weeks, I invited friends to my house to pray. Our prayers were mostly about seeking what's next. We wanted only what God wanted. We dropped our preferences to the floor and held empty hands up to the Lord.

After prayer, my mind changed about many things.

God's answer to those prayers was, "Wait."

Without a real job, it seemed I had no purpose. However, God showed me my purpose was the same whether I was doing it in the confines of a legitimate job or not. That purpose was to know God, make Him known and bring Him glory.

A new direction began to take form. I understood a paycheck didn't define my purpose. Nothing essential had changed. Things which seemed to be falling apart were falling into place. These extraordinary thoughts, which adjusted my thinking toward my circumstances, were the fruit of my long-standing faith and trust in God. I found promises in God's Word to speak to my fearful heart. One of my favorites is Isaiah 43:18-19:

> **"Forget the former things; do not dwell on the past. See, I am doing a new thing! Now it springs up; do you not perceive it? I am making a way in the wilderness and streams in the wasteland."**

NEW ADVENTURE

After working for so many years guiding others to a changed mind, this new direction seemed to be for my own benefit. Intellectually, I knew God uses setbacks to move us toward something better, but I was keenly aware there would be no paycheck at the end of the month and bills would come in. I began to understand that although my friends and I prayed for a job, the ultimate goal was to bring glory to God—job or no job. To be honest, I just couldn't see how anything could be fixed unless I was hired somewhere doing something. My sight was limited. God had other plans and He was about to rock my world. God was about to use His people to show me how to totally depend on Him. Jill was right. A harvest was coming, but not the one I was seeking.

A SHORT RETURN TO A CLOSED DOOR

September 2010, a wedding invitation at the site of my last job caused me to return to my sometimes still-hurt-feelings. It was awkward to return to that church. However, I wanted to honor my friend's daughter by attending and besides, it was about her, not me, so I went.

At first, I felt strange and uncomfortable entering that building again. What would people think of me? What if they asked about my new job? Did they even wonder why I was there? Eventually I realized no one was thinking those thoughts and I calmed down and enjoyed the wedding. I had needed to revisit that arena just to bring my feelings to a place of closure. My ministry at this place was finished and I no longer belonged there.

I could walk confidently into my future, wherever that would be. It became clearer and clearer that my ties to this job were over. It was time to mentally and emotionally move on. I could almost hear the Lord saying, "Move on. I've got your back!"

After obediently attending the wedding, I received a phone call that evening. Choosing to Excel (C2E) based in Conway, Arkansas, assembles several programs to help young people and their families make better choices for their lives. Thelma Moton, the director, asked me to speak on abstinence. She had grant money that had to be spent within a few weeks or she'd lose it, so I was hired to speak for two weeks. Because all my employment doors were closed, I was happy to be available to do this. I was overwhelmed with gratitude at this opportunity. It was as though God was whispering to me, "Relax. I am here."

Many friends called almost every day and often took me out to eat. At first, I was embarrassed.

When I told Thelma how I was thinking, she advised, "Let them. This is the fruit of your labor. This is their way of showing you love and support."

So, I traded my embarrassment for gratitude.

SOW A SEED

"We need a girls' basketball coach and I was wondering if you'd be interested in doing it," said my friend, whose child attended a local Christian school.

Of course I was interested!

They asked how much I needed to be paid. I called my friend, Temple, a college basketball coach, and asked her how much I should charge.

Surprisingly, she said, "You need to sow a seed."

I reminded her I was unemployed.

She just said it again, "You need to sow a seed."

Later that evening, I was listening to Tony Evans on television, and he said we should be about planting seeds. The next morning in my quiet time, there was the lesson again on planting seeds.

Remembering the Henry Blackaby's Bible study, Experiencing God, I realized what was happening. Blackaby's study encourages us, "Don't just do something. Stand there. Watch and see where God is working and join Him there."

The new, but stunning thought came thundering into my mind. God wants me to do this for free. I didn't understand this in the light of my bills. Still, wrestling with this revelation,

I called the school and told them, "I have to sow a seed, so I'll do it for free."

They were overwhelmed and grateful. Knowing my situation, they were awed I was willing to do this at no cost to them. Their acceptance of my offer gave me a sense of security, value, and worth. I didn't realize I hadn't been feeling those things until then. Now when people asked me what I was doing, I could tell them I was coaching at Word of Outreach School.

This began the journey with girls' basketball. It was my first time to coach, and I was nervous. On the first day when I entered the small gym, I realized the girls shared the gym with the boys, girls on one side, and boys on the other. Not only that, but there was no water and no basketballs. I was wondering how I would pay for these things myself. One Sunday, a lady in church quietly put some money my hand. Later when I looked at how much was there, I saw it was $10. Ungratefully, I thought, what am I going to do with this? Just what can I get for $10?

Suddenly, I stopped myself, "You big dummy. This is how you pay for the water."

I laughed, ashamed at my ingratitude, realizing the Lord had just told me, "I've got this and I'll take care of that."

This was a ministry opportunity and ministry can't stop even if there's no paycheck. If God is in it, He'll meet the needs.

This assignment gave me a purpose for each day. Although we didn't win even one game, the faculty, students, and parents treated me as someone important. Doing it for free spoke loudly to them. I enjoyed working with the students.

I thought I was through working with kids, but God had other plans for my future. He was testing my obedience. My commitment to obey Him was clear, even if it was for free.

BILLS PAID

"The Lord told my wife and me to pay your house payment and electric bill for the month of December," Jeff insisted.

Hesitating, I said, "I haven't run out of money yet."

"I didn't ask you if you'd run out of money yet," he said. "This is what the Lord told us to do. We want to do that for you."

Again, I ran through a range of emotions—embarrassment, shame, and incredible gratitude. I sensed the Lord was telling me again, "I got you."

During Christmas I went home to my family. My heart was so encouraged when my older brother unexpectedly looked me in the eye and said, "I don't have to worry about you because God always takes care of you." That made my heart smile.

Not only did God send friends to show encouragement, but my family was also a source of support. Sadly, I couldn't buy Christmas gifts for my nieces and nephews. This is something I loved doing. However, my family understood. One brother had some very specific ideas about what he thought I could use. Before too long, those things were in my possession. His support warmed my heart. My family embraced this season of unemployment with understanding grace.

SYRUP AND INTEGRITY

During those long months of "famine," the Lord allowed me to see His provision in January 2011. When resources were limited, every problem seemed enormous and insurmountable. One morning I awoke with a craving for pancakes, which was a rare treat for me. I could imagine the crispy edges, swimming in butter and syrup. When I looked in the cabinet for syrup, there was none. Disappointed, I took a quick trip to the store. I stood staring at different brands of syrup seeing their prices. I tried to figure out the best deal. The agony of deciding to buy or not to buy was taking a toll on me. I argued with myself about the real need of this $2.50 purchase. Did I want to spend the money, or should I do without? Such a dilemma. I've never in my life had to second guess such a small purchase. Eventually I walked out of that store with a small bottle of syrup and those pancakes tasted scrumptious.

When I was paring down my monthly expenses, I had discontinued paying the premium on my home warranty insurance. Sadly one morning I woke up to discover my microwave wasn't working. Now I needed the insurance. I called the insurance company to reinstate it.

They said, "If anything in your house is already broken, it won't be covered."

Seriously, the only reason I wanted to reinstate the policy was to report a broken microwave a few days later. I even made an appointment for them to come look at my microwave. My conscience got the best of me. My integrity wouldn't allow me to claim my broken microwave illegally. This experience showed me how easy it is to cut corners when your back is to the wall. I called the insurance company back and cancelled. A friend came over, looked at the microwave, and replaced a fuse! I thought my back was up against the wall, but now I realized my back was against God and I was leaning on Him.

CAUGHT OFF GUARD

Because my medical benefits would disappear soon, I made an appointment for a checkup. During that time, I explained my unemployment situation with my doctor and told him I had been caught off guard.

He said, "Caught off guard? Let me tell you about being caught off guard!" He shared he had lost his five-year-old daughter in a terrible accident. "How do you prepare for something like that?"

Listening to his heartbreaking story, my heart sank. I realized my situation was temporary and fixable, but his was permanent. Despite his tragedy, he said God was sovereign and in control of everything. This clear word from him put my situation in a proper perspective. God had used him to remind me it's only God who's in control, not me.

CHAPTER 14

NONPROFIT

CASTING A VISION

"You should be speaking full time!" Matt Mosler, a well known meteorologist and news anchor in Little Rock, had heard me speak at a leadership conference in the Delta several years before I became unemployed. I remember him running across the stage and enthusiastically saying he had never heard a purity message like this.

During this time of unemployment, I emailed Matt in hopes he might connect me to a possible job. When he heard I had no job, he encouraged, insisted even, that I should pursue a career in speaking full time.

Considering this outrageous idea was something I would've dismissed in the past. However, this new concept was something I began to explore through prayer and godly counselors. I considered this possibility as coming from the Lord. As this idea began to take shape, I became excited at the possibilities of doing something new for the Lord. On the other hand, I wondered just how to do it. Doubts tried to take me over. How do you get an audience? Who wants to hear me? How do I sell my self and my abilities? How in the world could this work? The thought of full-time speaking scared me.

Still, I could feel excitement at the possibility of teaching God's truth to young people. I love having such a focused mission that could change lives.

A couple came to me the following Sunday at church and said, "We heard you'll be speaking full time. You need a website to advertise."

I didn't understand why I needed a website. They explained a website created a path so people could contact me. I told them I had a friend who could put that together for me.

But they insisted, "No! You need to have it professionally done, and we'll pay for it!"

This out-of-the-blue offer shocked me. I felt so protected, so nurtured, so affirmed. This was an answer to a need I didn't even know I had.

Although I love speaking words of truth and life to groups, I wondered what else I should be doing. I wouldn't be speaking all the time. As I thought deep and long about this new direction, I mentioned it to a friend and she said, "You should start a non-profit organization."

In disbelief, I said, "We're in the middle of a recession. How in the world could that happen?"

"What will it hurt?" she said. "You're not doing anything else, anyway. (Ouch) If you were to start one, what would you do?"

I began to dream. Just what would I do if I directed a non-profit organization? All the things I had done before began to make sense. I wrote down three things that would take front and center of a non-profit: speaking, mentoring, and counseling. The more I thought about this, the more sense it made. But I didn't know where to start, who to call, what to do.

$850.00

By April 2011, I jumped into the process of applying for a 501C3 (non-profit) status, which proved to be intimidating. Form after form demanded my ideas take a definite shape. Filling out government paperwork was a foreign activity to me and I was afraid I was doing it wrong. Then I found out just applying for that status, required a fee of $850. Well, at this shaky stage of unemployment, I found that to be a brick wall. I had bills to pay. Realizing this fee stood between me and a completed application, I abandoned the whole idea.

Within a day I received a phone call from a couple who said, "We heard you're considering speaking full time and are applying for non-profit status. We want to pay the application fee!"

I thought this was just too much. Going forward on someone else's money was too much pressure. What if I wasn't granted the 501C3? The money would be gone and I'd feel as if it were my fault. When I expressed to the donors I was scared it wouldn't be granted and they'd lose their money, they assured me I shouldn't even be thinking like that. I needed several days to think and pray about this. During this wrestling time, God kept reminding me He was in control; my future was in His hands, and He and only He was sovereign. Three days later, I accepted their generous offer and moved forward with the process.

ABOVE WATER

My friends, the Fergusons, who had expertise in forming businesses and ministries, agreed to help me form a ministry strategy. After a series of meetings and lots of prayer, the non-profit organizational plan was committed to paper.

By this time, I had been unemployed for almost a year. Money was low. I had occasional speaking events and set up private basketball lessons, which helped keep my finances above water. God was taking care of me.

One time I opened a devotional book I kept by the sink in my bathroom and found $100. Another day, as I was riding my bike near a park, I looked down and saw wadded up dollar bills just lying around in random spots. I stopped and gathered them up. That $12 looked like a million bucks to me. Always, when I was bordering on slipping off my positive mindset, God sent a provision, just like he did for the Israelites in the desert. This was my manna. I stretched that money as far as it would go.

APPROVED

By August 2011, my money was running out and the 501C3 application was submitted. Many people asked if I had non-profit status yet because they wanted to donate to the ministry. I had heard it takes months and months for a non-profit to be approved, but Lessons for Life became a legal entity in September 2011. I took that miraculous movement of the government—only two months—as an affirmation from the Lord this was, indeed, His work and I had His approval.

The first Lessons for Life board consisted of Matt Mosler, Mark Leverett, Jerri Natali, and Lynn Pangburn Brunson. The early days were a time of our growing together, becoming knitted together around a common ministry that was being formed. As a unit, these precious people poured into me, encouraging me, constantly reminding me God was in the midst of this calling. Their support made me realize I wasn't carrying the heavy load by myself. My confidence began to settle and grow. At that point, they didn't fully understand the vision, but believed in me as I believed in God.

For my salary, they asked me, "How much money do you need to live?"

I answered, "I just need enough to pay my bills."

By this time, paying my bills dominated my mind, and my godly gratitude recognized this as abundance. Support began to arrive as people heard about this new venture to expose people to God's wisdom. Speaking invitations started to come in, requests came from various schools, youth organizations, churches and youth ministries. Lessons for Life was up and running. The desert of unemployment was behind me. Although relief flooded my heart, I still sensed an undercurrent of insecurity because everything was so unknown.

I occupied my mind with ideas for speaking engagements. I had no thoughts about a physical place for Lessons for Life. However, my board and my friends had eyes to see the need for this.

OFFICE SPACE

Although I was working out of my home and held meetings at my church, New Life Church, I shared with the board how I wished I could have a separate place to work. Ministry money was tight, and I would have been happy with a cubicle. After praying, a board member asked around and found someone who owned a space that had been vacant for a long time. When I was taken into the space by my board member, it was a small room with glass and three walls. This was thrilling to me, and I said, "This will be just fine."

"That's not all." She guided me into the next room, which was a huge open space that had a bathroom. The entire space covers 1400 square feet. Because this space had been used for storage for several years, the carpet was unusable, the walls were stained and a water leak caused a smell.

Overwhelmed, I said, "Oh, this is too much! What will I do with all that space?"

She told me, "I don't know. We'll have to see what God's going to do."

The outcome was I was given this space anonymously. I was overwhelmed and humbled by this generosity. To this day, I don't know who's responsible for this gift. God was showing me He was in favor of my moving forward with this nonprofit. Friends rallied and formed a team that painted the walls at no cost to the ministry. Another friend asked if his company could donate new carpet and tile. Again, God's people were setting the stage, and it was fabulous.

DÉCOR

"Just because you're a nonprofit doesn't mean you have to look like one." A friend made this comment after looking at the new office space. Generally, I keep things in order minimally, with little thought as to the beauty of a place.

My friend invited me to go shopping with her for furniture. As we moved amongst the pieces, she encouraged me to pick out what I liked. It took a while to just look at the furniture without making the price tag my priority. Her decorating abilities coupled with my limited "taste" resulted in a fully furnished office at no expense to the ministry. Another friend donated a beautiful brand-new table and chairs for meetings. Many others saw needs and met them. My office is a true show place. These precious ones were listening to God and responding, and I was so grateful. But they expressed gratitude that I was allowing them to do this. Even now, I am still astounded at all the beauty that surrounds me. It is a place of peace.

When anyone comes to my office, the outside small room holds a beautiful desk, two chairs, a table, colorful art and photos on the walls. The large inside room contains a large cream couch facing two comfy black chairs, separated by a coffee table. The conference table and chairs sit below oversized decorative art on the wall. Every wall holds canvas photos of ministry and mentoring events, as well as art pieces.

OPEN HOUSE

"I am so impressed with your office! God is blessing you!"

"We are so excited to see where God will take you and this ministry."

"We are behind you and will support you."

After completing the workplace, we held an open house in the new Lessons for Life office. I invited those friends who knew me and contributed to the ministry. My board also invited their friends who might be interested in supporting Lessons for Life. Over 100 people came to celebrate the beginning. Many were surprised at seeing friends there. Few realized how far-reaching the support was.

Seeing all those people who took time out of their day to celebrate with me at God's blessing and approval on Lessons for Life, filled me with humility. As I looked at all those faces, I sensed a real oneness of spirit and compassion. These people were entrusting the direction of this ministry to me by their willingness to help.

As we all crowded into the Lessons for Life office space, I explained the direction of this ministry (as far as I knew it), expressed gratitude to all who had provided for the completion of this beautiful office and encouraged those who had believed in me. Most of all, I made sure to give the glory to God. He was the One who provided through His obedient people. Rick Bezet, my pastor, graciously agreed to pray God's blessing for the building, the ministry, the volunteers, and me. Having the backing of my church was a priceless gift.

WARDROBE

"Now that you're speaking in public, you need to change your wardrobe. I know you have an event close to your birthday, so I want to buy you an outfit for your present. Meet me at the store after you get off work."

My taste in clothing has always been simple, but classy. Now I was given help in choosing. When I got to the store, my friend had already done a lot of shopping, and the basket was full!

She held up piece by piece, asking, "Do you like this one? How about this one?"

I was overwhelmed. After trying on several things, I chose one outfit. She kept asking if I liked the other pieces, too. I said I did, but I liked the one I had chosen.

"Well, we're just going to get everything in this basket and this will be your birthday present!"

My stunned embarrassment quickly gave way to gratitude. I went home with a whole new wardrobe and a grateful heart. Again, God was using His people to bring Him glory.

NEW CAR

My car was seven years old, paid for, and dependable. Another friend who was gifted with forward thinking, looked into my future and said, "Alexis, since you will be speaking all over the place and you'll be driving a lot, you might want to think about getting a new car."

I wasn't able to take on a car payment, so I just told her I liked my car and it worked. She insisted I go to her husband's dealership, look at cars and just listen to what the salesman had to say. So, I did. I looked at a lot of cars, deciding that because I carry around people and props, an SUV would be best, but I wasn't ready to sign anything.

The next day, I sat at a sporting event with this same lady, and she told me I should be getting a call on Monday concerning the car. She had prayed for her husband to lease the ministry a car without her bringing it up. Over dinner, he initiated a conversation and agreed to do that. God was speaking to His people, blessing me, and bringing Himself glory.

FOG (FAVOR OF GOD)

Entering my new office, my work nest in those early days, I sat at my desk looking over the beauty of my office, stunned. Walking into the meeting room, I was overwhelmed at what was there. The concept of "abundance" overtook my mind, followed closely by deep gratitude. None of this was of my doing; none of this was deserved. Over and over I saw things coming my way I didn't even know I needed. The work and things in my office are a daily reminder of the way God works.

> **"Give generously to them and do so without a grudging heart; then because of this the Lord your God will bless you in all your work and in everything you put your hand to." Deuteronomy 15:10**

It was so clear to me that those who had given to Lessons for Life had done so without a "grudging heart," but rather with a grateful heart, pleased at being able to do so. They will experience God's blessing on their work. I, too, had given generously and found God's blessing. It seemed like I was standing on the starting line of a brand new race, ready to go, fully prepared. The stage was set. Now I had to watch with eternal eyes where the Lord would lead me. As things began to unfold, the path before me took some surprising turns.

This "nest" affirms to me God has me right where I belong. Only God's sovereign hand could have assembled this new life for me. To God be the Glory!

CHAPTER 15

L4L-MENTORING

ONE-ON-ONE

"What kind of school is this?" I asked. I knew what this place was but wanted to have a conversation. "Is it preparing you for college? Or a profession?"

"Of course not," the Alternative School students responded. They explained students were placed at this school after fighting, truancy, or insubordination, etc. This was one step away from the Juvenile Detention Center.

Because all my speaking requests were for weekends, I was free to do other things during the weekdays. I believed the Lord was telling me to serve in a local public school. A few weeks prior to this meeting, I entered the Alternative School to offer them a mentoring program for their girls. Walking into the Alternative School was a true step of faith. Because I am always drawn to the troubled girls, and because of my background, I sensed God was leading me to that school. God had put a strong passion in my heart for the kids who were hardest to reach.

The principal passed me on to the assistant principal, saying, "You talk to this lady. She wants to start a mentoring program, and I don't have time to meet with her."

Darlene Little-Knighten agreed to speak with me. After listening, she said, "I was already thinking about doing something for the girls. I think this is the right thing!"

I submitted a rough plan. We decided to mentor during the students' lunch time. However, before inviting any mentors into this school, Kim Tramel, my faithful friend who walks with me into many ministry places, and I asked to be allowed to sit in the back of some classrooms to observe. We came for one week and saw what the teens were like. We saw beautiful students with ugly behavior. They showed incredible disrespect to their teachers and to each other. We realized teachers had to address disciplinary issues more than teaching. This observation time confirmed we were right to come to this school.

c. 2021. Mentor Bryan celebrates a successful year with Zoe. Left to Right: Bryan Dietz, Zoe Saine, Alexis Ware.

Interestingly, each teacher asked, "Miss Ware, do you have anything to say to the class?"

Surprised, I began to dialogue with them about why they were in this school. After hearing from them, I calmly said, "You choose your way, but you cannot choose your consequences. All choices have consequences, good or bad."

"For example, I have a nonprofit organization, and we need money. When I leave your class, I'm going to the bank to rob it. Pretty sure I'll get caught. I'll just tell them to put me on probation. We all know that's not going to happen. When I made the choice to rob the bank, I gave up my right to choose the consequence."

The students' nodding heads showed they had grasped the concept. The students' attentiveness and interest affirmed my desire to start a mentoring program at that school. Also, the teachers in the room were stunned to see how the students engaged with me.

Kim and I skipped the next week but came back the following week.

One student came up to me and said, "Where've you been?"

This simple comment also confirmed to me I was in the right place at the right time. This made the decision to bring mentoring into this school clear.

I soon realized all I was told about alternative school teens was wrong. Although we saw them getting in trouble left and right, we realized they were crying out for help, understanding, acceptance and for someone to care about them. That was right up my alley.

The next step was to approach my circle of friends. I told them, "I want to start a mentoring program."

"We want to be part of that," they said. "Give us the details."

As friends told other friends, sixteen mentors came forth. Most of those women knew me and trusted I wouldn't steer them wrong. They witnessed God blessing my efforts, and they wanted to take part. This immediate and willing positive response gave me encouragement.

The mentoring program was taking shape. A new journey was beginning. Before the mentoring program began, I assembled a short mentor training. I knew most of these women had never faced working with struggling urban teens. However, we were all walking into a new adventure together. The common thread was we all had strong relationships with Jesus Christ. We were willing to walk with faith through the door He opened.

Because I didn't know the teen girls or the mentors personally, God intervened in matching them up. The girls were chosen by Mrs. Little-Knighten, the assistant principal. They were willing to participate in the program. I paired them with their new mentors. Excitement filled me. There were so many details, new mentors, meeting new students and just a day full of unknowns. The first day, nervous, but eager mentors arrived. I prepared them by going over the meeting agenda and praying for their first time with the girls.

As the students came through the door and gave me their signed parent permission slips, I introduced them to their individual mentors. They had been encouraged to ask ice-breaker type questions while they waited for the meeting to start. No one knew I was as nervous and awkward as everyone else, but I had to guide them. I was looking at a room full of risk-takers. We started with games and everyone began to relax. The girls' excitement was contagious. We all sensed how thrilled they were to finally be in a room where they weren't in trouble, but rather encouraged.

This was the Alternative School, so we couldn't predict how the girls would respond to this new club. Surprisingly, they willingly came each week, bringing their school lunch, to meet with their mentors and hear a lesson from me. The school was puzzled because there were no discipline problems during mentoring time. Each week, various faculty members expressed gratitude to us for coming and loving their students. I helped them realize we were meeting a need all teens have for a loving caring adult involved in their lives. The first year was a success for the school, mentors, girls, and for me.

CENSORING MENTORS

"Alexis, I'm going to take my girl home!" Jen said.

"You're taking WHO?" I asked.

"I'm taking my mentee home with me," Jen said.

"You've lost your mind," I said. "You can't take any of these kids home."

"My girl is pregnant, and she can't take care of a baby by herself."

Sarcastically I told Jen, "You can, but when you do, you'll take her family home, too. And her boyfriend. Then you'll need to be responsible for her to meet the requirements of probation. That'll come into your house, too. Do you want that?"

"Well, no," she said.

"Boundaries allow you freedom to love without strings," I said. "Just come here once a week and offer her hope and love. You're not the solution to all the bad choices she's made, or the ones made for her. You can't fix any of it. It is what it is. Just love her here and now. You're here for a reason, at this time, for this girl, so the Lord is ordering it all. Otherwise, you would've never met her. Don't lose sight of why we are here."

COACHING MENTORS

Bursting into tears a mentor melted down in front of me. "I can't do this!"

"What's wrong?" I asked.

"I feel the heaviness of this place," she said. "It's oppressive. It's so sad for these kids."

Agreeing, I said, "God has us here for a purpose."

Every week, I prayed with the mentors before the students came. I helped them understand our mission was to take light and love into that darkness. That burdened mentor faithfully continued mentoring for the rest of the year. She took on the burden as an opportunity to love her mentee. Within the boundaries drawn around her, she loved her mentee well.

Every mentoring day, when I spoke briefly to the mentors to prepare them for the time with their student, many took what they learned through the program back to their own families. They were applying what they'd learned. Some mentors said it helped them personally in their walk with the Lord.

One even said, "That devotional time is my favorite time of the week!"

ALTERNATIVE SCHOOL GRADUATION

I slammed my brand-new white Nike shoe onto the stage. THUMP!

The unruly audience was shocked into silence. I knew this would get their attention because everybody valued that white Nike.

Because I was at the Alternative School weekly during the school year, they invited me to be the graduation speaker. However, the atmosphere in the cafeteria was disruptive and chaotic. Other speakers and important school officials were disrespected routinely, so I was worried about being humiliated. How would they respond to me? But I wouldn't back down from my commitment. Before I came on stage, the audience wouldn't settle down. They introduced me, but no one seemed to notice. So, after I threw that shoe, the audience quieted into a shocked silence.

The thrown shoe led into my story about a young man who had experienced the same thing. When he was a little boy someone threw his brand-new shoe into the dirt, and to this day, he still holds a grudge. He won't let this go. This was an example of how you can let your past keep dictating your future, even when the original issues are long gone. Knowing most of those students came out of difficult backgrounds, I told them their past didn't need to predict their future. Students and their families were attentive during my talk and I perceived a supernatural peace confirming the Lord had used this message. But when I left the stage, chaos arose again.

After two years at the Alternative School, a mentor suggested we begin the mentoring program with younger students at a middle school. I loved being in the Alternative School, but there was also the thought if we mentored the girls earlier in their lives, maybe they wouldn't end up in the Alternative School. Our Lessons for Life mentoring program moved the next year into a local middle school.

HENDERSON MENTORING

"Ms. Alexis Ware is my role model because she is such an inspiration. She does things I wish to do. She's flown all over the state. While she was traveling, she spread the gospel. She abides in her religion and her relationship with God, and she loves to teach about God and how to become a better Christian and more. That's what I'd like to spend my life doing too."

One of my middle school girls surprised and humbled me by writing about me for her English assignment: The assignment was to write an essay about a role model in your life. Her words confirmed I was still in the right place doing the right things.

Later in the year, she said, "Ms. Alexis has this energy and this way of getting her words to speak to you. Her words cut you so deep, you want to listen. She can teach a lesson out of anything."

Concerning her mentor, this student said, "I'm very private and a lot of the time I'm all closed doors...it's like she kicked those doors right open. I didn't feel like I needed to keep information from her...she had ears to listen."

About her growing relationship with God, she said, "I can't say I've known God. I've surely known OF Him. Ms. Alexis is...

so passionate about the Lord, that you can't do anything but aspire to have a faith like hers...She...showed me the life of camp at KAA, where I learned to love God...and praise Him...KAA is where I got saved. Ms. Alexis has helped me to get my faith to where it is now and she's still helping me grow in my faith."

BUILDING MENTORS TOO

Monthly, I gave the mentors a verse to commit to memory.

> **"Give me wisdom and knowledge, that I may lead this people, for who is able to govern this great people of yours?"**
> **2 Chronicles 1:10**

I encouraged the mentors to pray these words for themselves: wisdom, and knowledge over their girls, over their homes, over their marriages and over those who cross their paths. I also wanted them to view their girls as great people, gifts from God. Many mentors have shared with me how much memorizing verses had meant to them. Some have even taken verses into their workplaces and shared with co-workers.

One mentor who served several years, had a challenging student who came from a difficult background. As a 6th grader, she was shy, but by 7th grade, she was befriended by a destructive girl and the relationship was evidenced by a drastic change of attitude. She went from shy to surly and began to buck authority. She acted as if she didn't want to learn anything directly, but she knew her mentor had three daughters, so she would open the door to wisdom by asking, "What would you tell your daughters about this?"

Meanwhile, her weekly meetings with her faithful mentor continued. I watched as this godly wise woman truly understood the attitude change was not her fault. She was in a position to speak words of life into the girl and point her to God. She kept a proper perspective and saw this girl's needs more than her poor behavior. She planted seeds of truth and explained often that things could be very different simply by making different choices. By 8th grade the negative friend was gone, and the student's attitude improved. The mentor and the girl enjoyed a season of stability together. My heart is warmed personally when I see a mentor with the right perspective interact with a child who doesn't respond well but the mentor continues to persevere.

When the program concluded at the end of the school year, we had a big celebration because the students had completed something good. Because these girls rarely met with success, finishing anything was truly cause for celebration. Several volunteers came early to decorate tables and set out catered food. A gift table held a surprise for each girl from Lessons for Life. The whole room was a party, a true celebration.

There was a share time when the girls could verbalize what they learned. In this kind of set up, we never knew how impactful this season was until the sharing began. I was always especially curious to hear these testimonies, because I wasn't working directly with the girls. The mentors and I were stunned and pleased when we heard the girls express these thoughts of things they had absorbed.

I am valuable, worthy, beautiful.

I learned that I am loved even if I don't think that about myself.

I matter every day.

I need to focus on what's important.

I need to let people in.

I need to control myself during peer pressure. Handle stuff in a positive way.

I don't have to let my past predict my future.

As the girls expressed to their mentors how important this little once-a-week mentoring meeting had become to them, many times the mentors were stunned and blessed immensely.

Each girl was encouraged by the principal to write a note to their mentor expressing gratitude. I encouraged each mentor to purchase a journal to give to their girl. The first page was for their note of encouragement to their student. As the notes and journals were exchanged, tears began to flow all around the room. Some mentors heard for the first time their girl loved them. Some girls read words of hope for a bright future. At this time every year, I stand at the front of the room watching this great exchange.

This celebration warms my heart to watch something so precious develop. I remembered the insecurity of each girl when we began the year. Some walked into the room battling shyness; never raising their hand to answer a question. After being encouraged by their mentors all year, discussions became animated. Most wanted to share. Others walked into the Lessons for Life room full of suspicion, not knowing if they could trust the mentors. As the year went on, I witnessed a growing maturity. Awkwardness was replaced by trust. This day I heard growth and maturity as the girls grasped lessons they were taught. They were journeying to a new confidence.

Because God had moved me from insecurity to security, I was able to understand and nurture the journey in these girls and mentors. My gratitude to the Lord overwhelms me as I witness His work every year.

Ms. Little-Knighten commented, "Many of our students are in a state of crisis. Some are the parent for other siblings while mom is at work. Some live in poverty-level environments. A few are living without parents (deceased). Others may suffer from grief, anxiety, depression and instability." Her support for Lessons for Life is invaluable. She said, "This program has a tremendous impact on my girls because it reminds them...they are important,...of value and worth. I can see the difference in that my girls are becoming more mature, learning how to make better decisions...A program like this is actually needed in all of our schools."

MY MENTORS: LOSS

Jill, my mentor, contracted cancer and passed away February 13, 2013 in her early 50s. Jill's absence on this earth was a time of emotional shaking for me. I experienced little grief in my life, so I wasn't sure how I was supposed to feel or be. This was the first time someone who was deeply connected to me had passed away. I was uncomfortable with my swirling emotions. We had prayed passionately and diligently for Jill's healing, and yet she died. I believed God answered prayers and her passing was that answer. My concept of healing enlarged to conclude that entering heaven is the ultimate healing.

Her death also required I face my mortality. Death would also be my end on earth. I was living each day as though I had an unlimited number in front of me. Putting a framework of death around my days made them more precious and required a more deliberate kind of living. There would be an end to my days, just as Jill's days had ended.

For her last birthday, Jill invited her friends to a party. Always a giver, Jill gave a gift to everyone present. It was a small plastic high-heeled shoe. It represented her desire for us to "step it up." She encouraged us to take our spiritual walk seriously and move into ministry wherever we were. Her legacy was to keep moving, serving, honoring our Lord with our lives while we still had them.

The Lord showed me through other grieving friends it was fine to be sad, but it shouldn't consume me. As I walked through the following days without Jill's counsel, God had given me more days to serve Him and I needed to be about His business.

The earthly loss of Jill coupled with her mission message gave me the capacity to continue God's work.

A NEW MENTOR

"Alexis, we really loved your presentation. We really loved what you had to share. Do you have a card?" Jan and her husband stood in line to talk with me.

Others were waiting to talk with me, so they took my card and moved on. I was the keynote speaker at a youth conference in Houston, Texas. That night, Jan texted me to restate her encouragement.

The next morning she called me and apologetically said, "I passed your information on to our youth pastor, so you can expect a call from him. I hope that was all right."

I thanked her, but considered our involvement finished.

However, days later, Jan called me and said, "God has placed you on my heart and I believe He wants me to help you get to the next place in your ministry."

In my mind, I thought she might find me more speaking venues, but that wasn't what she meant. She went on, expressing a desire to pour into my life. My guard went up. She was younger than I, lived in Austin, Texas, and I lived in Arkansas. But, the Lord gave me a peace about this growing friendship, so we stayed in contact through telephone calls.

As months passed, we talked occasionally and became acquainted. Jan's calls began to mean more and more to me and I began to trust her. It had been two years since Jill's passing. God began to knit my heart with Jan's. We discovered her ministry, Kids' Life, and mine, Lessons for Life, were both based in our love for children. She was drawn to my bent for translating God's Word so young people could understand it. God had graciously gifted me with another mentor.

"Every good and perfect gift is from above, coming down from the Father of the heavenly lights, who does not change like shifting shadows." James 1:17a

Jan was a perfect gift from God. She was a neutral voice and a discerning spirit. I could share situations with her, and she immediately saw God's hand, direction and provision. She responded with grace and no judgment.

As I spoke in various venues, Jan told me to call her right before I got on stage, so she could pray for me. No one had ever offered to do that before. Jan spoke words of wisdom to me many times without knowing how impactful they were or appropriate to the situation.

Eventually, she pointed out to me, "Alexis, people don't really know you. You never share your personal struggles when you speak."

This took me by surprise, but as I thought about it, I realized she was right. As I spoke to a different group one day, I unintentionally finished early. With several minutes left, I considered how to use this extra time. Jan's words came back to me. I began to share some of my life challenges and how the Lord used them. This kind of vulnerability made me feel naked, exposed and uncomfortable.

Afterwards, an adult came up to me, weeping, to thank me. This was an affirmation God wanted me to use my struggles and His victories to help others.

Jan had told me, "God wants to take you to a new place in your ministry."

This kind of openness was strange for me, but when I saw the audience identifying with me, I gained confidence to share more. This was a turning point in Lessons for Life. My lesson examples took on a new reality.

The surprising benefit this brought to my life was amazing. Suddenly, personal issues took on deeper meanings as I revisited them, looking for the lesson.

When asked to share her side of this story, Jan responded, "Since our first conversation, God showed me [Alexis] had built walls around [herself], to guard her heart from being hurt. God gave her peace with me, and she shared one story at a time, not knowing how I would respond. Through every conversation, I showed her God's love, grace and mercy and that's when her trust began. I saw God raising her up to higher levels in her ministry, but she needed to be more transparent and share stories about herself.

"Feeling uncertain about sharing her life challenges, she shared first with one person, then went to her mentors, and finally she shared a story at one of her conferences. Text messages, letters, notes, emails [reveal] how much her message... changed their lives. She began to shift her focus [off herself and onto] God's people [pointing them to Him].

"... I am honored Alexis calls me one of her mentors, [but] she too has been a mentor to me, always speaking God's truth. Alexis is the most unselfish, Godly woman, prayer warrior, inspiring person I know."

The Lord knew as I walked willingly into the world of being a giver, I needed encouragement and support, so He sent Jan, who encouraged me to come out of hiding. The right woman with the right heart at the right time.

CHAPTER 16

INTERNATIONAL

HAITI

"Are you interested in going to Haiti?" a woman from church asked.

"Yes, why?" I asked.

"Someone would like to pay your way," she said.

"No way!"

The women of my church were invited to minister to orphans and widows in Haiti. Something stirred in my heart, and I had a strangely strong desire to go. When someone offered to pay my way, I was stunned. Why would somebody do this for me? Excitement filled me with joy, because I had done nothing to earn this trip.Yet somehow, I knew I should go. I didn't know why.

I attended the preparation meeting and received a handout describing what we needed to take with us. I didn't bother to look at it until the group began to pray. The item that stopped me in my tracks was that we could only bring two or three pairs of underwear. No way could I go through a week with only two or three pairs. While the rest of the group was praying, I was trying to figure out how to smuggle more underwear, even considering wearing seven pair at once.

After prayer, I realized I'd only seen the short list of items for our carry-on, not the full list. When I shared with the group my underwear plan, everyone had a great laugh.

Two weeks later as I boarded the plane, my heart was filled with excitement. We scheduled this trip a year after a terrible earthquake had devastated much of Haiti. That earthquake measured 7.5 on the Richter Scale, followed by 52 aftershocks (4.5+) over the next ten days. Approximately three million people were affected by the earthquake, with deaths ranging from 100,000 to 160,000. The needs were many. I didn't understand what I was about to find, so I was eager to walk into the unfamiliar.

Half of our group consisted of leadership women I highly respected. Also significant to me was for the first time, I entered a country where I was among the racial majority. Within our group I was the only black woman, but in Haiti, I just looked like everyone else, and my group was in the minority.

People had questioned us before we left about the lack of police protection in Haiti and the dangers there. But somehow, I felt safe, almost at home. My true security was in Christ who had called me to Haiti.

We landed in the tiny Haitian airport at Port Au Prince. Before we disembarked the airplane, they told us to not make eye contact, not to allow anyone to touch our luggage; just to walk straight to our mission vehicle. We didn't understand these orders till we exited the plane and people swarmed us wanting to carry our luggage so they could earn a tip. Leaving the airport, we walked through rows of taxi drivers begging for our business. We all walked, eyes looking straight ahead, to our awaiting van and boarded it.

On our way to the mission, we drove through areas of destruction left by the earthquake. We saw shacks, little shops and crowds of people. The sea of blue tents held displaced families who still had no place to live after a year. We drove past a huge pile of dirt holding a few crosses, a mass grave for those killed in the earthquake. The bus stopped when it reached Mission of Hope Ministry. This colorful compound including a kitchen building, a basketball court, dorms for guests, orphan shelters, a school, and a church, all painted in pastel colors. The evidence of earthquake deaths we just witnessed, caused our arrival to be silent as each of us processed what we'd just seen.

The first full day in Haiti, we went to a church service. When we arrived, church was already well underway. Because this was the highlight of the week for the Haitians, everyone was there, dressed in suits and dresses. The music was slightly familiar to me, and I realized I knew the song. Despite the language barrier, when the Haitians sang praises to the Lord, our team knew we were in God's presence. Although we knew the melody, but not the words, there was no mistaking what was happening. Watching the Haitians passionately crying out to the Lord drew me into genuine praise. There was a freedom to honor the Lord, however that looked. The comparison between people in deep poverty worshiping the God who has provided for them vs. American Christians who have so much and praise so little, was startling. Humbled, I questioned myself: Am I worshiping God because of who He is or because of what He's given me? This challenged me to take a second look at the reason behind my worship.

Over the next week, we took part in painting projects, sang with the orphans who lived on the compound and conducted a women's conference. We also provided a few craft projects for the Haitian women. One was simply making a necklace using pearl beads. When they were finished, the women were so proud. Several quietly placed them in their Bibles to keep them safe.

I enjoyed all my interaction with these precious people. Each day differed from the day before, and my heart was pierced with a new desire to love God's people. One of our projects was cleaning their small homes. After we swept and mopped the cement floors, wiped down counters and made beds, often the women wanted us to sing with them. Each day my heart was surprisingly touched.

Our food was fine, but I found out a lot of the meat was goat. That was just too much for me, so I secretly ate the protein bars, peanut butter crackers, and chips I brought.

The final day, parting tears flowed between the Haitians and our group. As I sat on the bus to return to the airport, the tears began to flow for me too, but for a different reason. These tears were for the new message I heard from the Lord: "Your passion for ministry had died." This startling thought crashed through all the other emotions I was feeling at that moment.

However, I also heard, "I have restored it!"

I cried even harder. God brought me to Haiti, not just for the mission, but to resurrect my hunger to serve Him. I headed home with a renewed passion for Lessons for Life.

ANOTHER TRIP TO HAITI

"Do you have everything for your trip?" my friend's husband asked me after church.

"Yes," I said. "I have everything I need."

He repeated, "Do you have everything?"

I looked at his wife and said, "Tell your husband I have everything I need."

She looked at me and replied, "I won't tell him anything. God must have put something on his heart."

"Do you have money for the trip?" he asked.

I said, "I'm all right."

I had a speaking invitation in Haiti. Hosean International Ministries, a non-profit Christian ministry teaching life skills and educational training, wanted to pay for my flight and housing. I accepted the request, excited at the prospect of speaking overseas. In thinking about personal needs for the trip, I realized I didn't have money for extras. When purchasing things for the trip, I was frugal. I found some shoes at a good price and purchased them. I struggled to figure out what to buy in the way of food, snacks, gear, etc. I visited the "not fair" mindset, wondering why the Lord would call me to do something, then not provide for it.

My friend sitting beside me had her hand on my back, praying for me. She seemed to sense a burden for me, but I hadn't told her much. Her silent prayer made me feel God was covering me.

After her husband questioned me about my needs, he looked at her and told her to write a check. She quickly did. Then he looked at it and said, "Add another zero to that." He asked what I had already bought, so I told him.

He said, "Take everything back, get your money refunded and use this."

Amazed and pleased, I took that check!

Finally, I was learning how to gracefully accept surprise gifts. Walking out of church that day, I was to-the-max joyful and couldn't wait to exchange everything. I remembered my negative "not fair" thoughts of the day before. To see God's hand continually moving on my behalf made me ashamed of going down that road again. I was learning my security, my peace and my maturity was changing, acknowledging God's hand on my life as He provides over and over again.

I took that check to the bank, barely looking at it, just seeing a five and a few zeros, and deposited it in my account. A few months later I got a notice from my bank saying I wrote $500 on my deposit slip, but the check was for $5000. This meant I had $4500 more than I had thought.

I texted my friends and said, "Wow! I just can't believe this!"

They had blessed the ministry in those early days. Again, I was honored and humbled.

My time in Haiti was spent speaking about purity to hundreds of children and young people at a camp run by Hosean International Ministries. This campground contained guest dorms, program buildings and a gazebo of rock with a thatched roof. Many buildings were open-air, meaning there was a dirt or concrete floor, half walls of painted stucco or rock and a roof. The young people were so enthusiastic and embraced everything I taught. All the talks had interaction, and everyone wanted to take part.

Because the Haitians spoke mostly Haitian Creole, I was assigned a translator. My speaking method is passionate and animated. Rose, our 26-year-old translator, interpreted with animation as well. However, as my message progressed, her animation decreased. This disturbed me because the audience could only understand her, and she was giving out an important message in an understated way. The audience began to disengage. My heart dropped. Another leader saw what was happening, so he quietly switched positions with her and picked up where she left off, and we finished strong.

Because I had more talks to give, and she was my assigned translator, I needed to understand what had happened. I was concerned we might have another disinterested audience again.

Later that day, I asked her, "Are you all right?"

"Yes."

"Well, something happened while I was speaking. It was like your demeanor changed."

I needed to spend some time with her one-on-one. She told me she had intended to stay a virgin till she was married, but through deception, her boyfriend had crossed that line with her a year ago. He tricked her by telling her he'd heard she was cheating on him. She insisted that she wasn't. He said she should have sex with him to prove she wasn't cheating. Her emotional state overtook her, and she gave in.

She was guilt-ridden, broken and ashamed. Tears of regret flowed down her face.

c. 2016. After speaking at a school, Alexis is surrounded by African students. The boy on the right said, "You remind me of my momma!"

I asked her, "Did you ask the Lord to forgive you?"

"Yes, but I can't let go of the disappointment."

I spent some time consoling her, encouraging her to walk in the forgiveness, reminding her that she had a testimony to share. As we talked, I sensed a release from the bondage of that guilt. God had brought me all the way from America to share His love and forgiveness with this precious Haitian girl. The rest of the time in Haiti, she translated with passion and freedom and a growing peace.

AFRICA

"Alexis, we read in your newsletter you might go to Africa," a friend said. "Are you still intending to go?"

Surprised, I responded, "Yes."

"We want to pay for the whole trip. Please send me the details of all the expenses and we'll cover it."

Immediately, I called my mom, with another "you-won't-believe-this" story.

c. 2016. Alexis with two African kids playing in their yard.

For years I had been dreaming of going to Africa. I didn't know why, but there was a definite desire to do that. Abby Fegtly, a Little Rock teen founded Blue Door Sponsorship which provides sponsors for children to attend school in Africa. Karman, Abby's mother, asked if I'd go with their group to Nairobi to speak to teens and staff. Thrilled, I put this request before the

Lessons for Life board, and they unanimously agreed that I should go.

For sure, God was in this. I eagerly moved forward, bought tickets, packed bags and left for the Dark Continent.

When I exited the plane in Nairobi, there were no words to express how ecstatic I was to be there. An unnatural anticipation overwhelmed me and I was strangely at home. Although locals gave us extensive rules for safety, I didn't feel afraid. Looking around, I just wanted to absorb the country and not miss a thing. Nairobi was a modern city with high-rise buildings. Extreme poverty was peppered throughout the city. Next to a sturdy rock or stucco home would be a hut with pieces of aluminum fastened to a fallen-in mud wall.

We drove through semi-modern streets that faded into a primitive world. Ditches of sewage paralleled the road. Pavement turned to dirt. Trash was scattered everywhere; some stuck in fences where the wind had carried it.

Our first full day in Nairobi, Kenya, was Sunday, so we attended church for hours. The worshipers had dressed in their best clothes then walked sometimes miles in the heat to attend church. Most came drenched in sweat, but ready to worship God. Although I didn't understand the language, the music was mostly percussion. I was in awe watching the worshipers move enthusiastically to repetitious words and a strong beat. Hands waved, feet moved and voices raised praises to the Lord. I was so excited when a familiar song was chosen, I sang loudly with abandon in my own language, joining with everyone, sensing God's presence. There was a freedom to worship that was new to me. It differed greatly from our American church format, schedules and time constraints. Humbled, I realized I had just worshiped God for who He is rather than for what He has done for me.

The next day the mission planned for our team to see different living situations in Nairobi and the whole poverty picture of the people we were about to serve. We visited different impoverished neighborhoods and ended in a place called The Base.

The Base may be the saddest place on earth. This dreadful location is where hundreds of orphaned teens gathered and sometimes lived. Their sole daily objective was to sniff fumes from a mixture of glue and jet fuel. These starving children spent their days begging for pennies which they used to purchase more of this concoction. Stoned, they could forget their hunger and the pointlessness of their lives. We were warned we might even find a newborn baby laying on the ground, because sometimes that happened. Fortunately, we didn't see that. Our purpose there was to see the dead end where hopelessness could lead. As we boarded the van to leave and the door was shut, a few teens walked to the door and gently tried to get in. They tried to show they wanted to go with us. Driving away, my heart was broken and a sadness swept through the whole bus.

When our team left, a sober shocked silence engulfed us. We were processing what we had just seen. The horror and pointlessness of life in that place of terrible oppression revealed a darkness we could never comprehend. I was frozen in disbelief as I realized I couldn't help them. Their hopelessness had somehow disarmed me. All I could do was to lay them on the altar before the Lord.

My original assignment was to speak to middle and high school students about purity. Before going to Africa, I considered how to change my abstinence talk to address this culture. As time grew near for me to share, Karman, our group leader, said I should keep the message the same.

My message reminded the students their bodies were the temple of the Holy Spirit, and should be treated with respect. I reaffirmed that God loved them, even if there had been sexual sin in the past. Also, I especially encouraged those who had been violated and reiterated that it wasn't their fault. Most students said they had never heard a purity message before. This was a whole new way of thinking. The teaching shocked even the teen boys. I spoke with confidence, but my prayer was for those who heard, that they'd hear the truth.

After speaking, seventeen-year-old Ayana, weeping and broken, wanted to speak with me, so we found a quiet room. The horrendous process of genital mutilation was rampant in her culture, and she endured this as a young child. It was expected that girls have sex with any man after undergoing that, so she did. For her, having random sex with any man became a normal way of life. Although she was an older teenager and could have the option of turning down sex, her culture and history hid that option from her. However, what I shared had broken something in her. That day Ayana heard hope and choice in my story.

She grabbed both my hands in hers, looked me in the eye and spoke with great passion, "I will never again have sex until I am married. I promise you, and I promise God." I heard her story, her promise and her newfound freedom with a deeply humble heart. Without a doubt, my trip to Africa was for her.

CHAPTER 17

MESSAGE

PRE-PROM CHALLENGE

Amidst lowered lights and wedding music, I entered the center aisle of the school assembly and reverently walked up to the stage, matching the rhythm of the music, and singing a beautiful wedding song. The ball gown skirt of my wedding dress swished between the aisles. Guys and girls stood quietly and respectfully as if this were a real wedding with a real bride passing by. A few students were even showing visible emotion including crying.

This was the week before prom, and I was invited to speak to local Christian high school students about purity. I spoke about choosing high standards and forming boundaries in relationships to protect those standards. This came directly from my college experience. The purity message was a sensitive issue, not only for the students, but for me as well. Always there was an emotional toll when I chose to become vulnerable to a roomful of people I didn't know.

I began to play with my skirt of many layers. As I lifted one layer, it exposed a boy's name, illustrating someone I supposedly had sex with. The audience gasped, and a few snickered.

c. 2014. Alexis singing in a wedding dress as part of her abstinence talk.

Another layer, another name. Another layer, yet another name. This was to drive home what happens when someone has sex before marriage and how crowded that marriage bed can be. It also shows how STD's (sexually transmitted diseases) can pass from one partner to another.

One of the students said, "That's the best purity talk we've ever had!"

Another said, "In her presentation, nobody was sleeping. Everybody's just tuned in, waiting to hear what she had to say next. I loved her presentation!"

These reactions fanned the fire within me to continue to share this desperately needed message. Students, staff and friends were present and influenced by this clear and powerful message of purity. It was then that I realized the deep impact my testimony had.

Because of this talk, they presented me with a contract position at the school to speak ten times a year at their chapel and to counsel students. Invitations came from other people and organizations just by word of mouth. I was humbled, honored and surprised that my story on purity was so impactful.

MAN DOWN

"Man down! Man down!"

When anyone in the military hears those words, it means someone is injured and needs help. It is a call to help. I told kids when they see a bullying situation, they needed to respond, "Man Down!" They should come to the aid of the injured party.

To illustrate, I asked several students to hold up signs showing different responses of the one being bullied, such as anxiety, loneliness, low self-esteem, depression, social withdrawal, refusal to go to school, absenteeism, poor academic performance, health complaints, running away from home, drugs, alcohol and finally, suicide. This showed how a bullying moment can have dire consequences. I encouraged the students to come quickly to the aid of the offended one. Also, I addressed the needs of the bully as well, acknowledging his internal struggles, his own insecurities, his need to cut someone else down in order to build himself up. I acknowledged both sides believed lies, and I was in a position to give them truth.

After I finished and the students were leaving, a young lady came up to me privately, held out her wounded arm and told me she was cutting herself because she was a victim of bullying. Although she was in counseling for this, she just wanted me to know. She could relate to what I said. I encouraged her to understand her own worth. Walking away from there, I was stunned at the impact this simple message was having.

PORN STAR?

"I am the first virgin porn star you'll ever meet!" I said laughing.

My friend who invited me to speak about purity twice to a secondary school in Oklahoma said, "You mean you're not offended by this? It was all over Facebook."

"The person described does not fit my character. Why would I be offended?"

He exhaled in relief. He requested I speak in his town in the school, even though there was a lot of racial tension there. He believed inviting me might break down some of the barriers.

Days before that phone call, I entered the school somewhat fearful before my speaking time and prayed for God to ease that tension. As the students entered the gym, they stared at me, puzzled and suspicious, wondering who I was.

Clearly and surprisingly, I sensed the Lord leading me to play the popular song, "The Whip."

I didn't have this song on my phone, didn't want it, but I felt the tug of the Lord to download it. As soon as the song began to play, the ice was broken. All the kids knew the motions to the senseless lyrics.

"Now watch me whip, watch me Nae Nae, Now watch me whip whip, watch me Nae Nae."

The students jumped up out of their seats and joined me on the gym floor, whipping and Nae Naeing all over the place. I laughed out loud, pleased they were all suddenly on board with me. When I stopped the song, they all reentered the bleachers, but I had their attention.

I introduced myself as Alexis from Texas and shared my personal purity story. The students were all ears for the rest of my presentation. Afterwards, many students bombarded me, expressing appreciation for the message and desiring pictures with me. One student went home and excitedly told his mom he had heard a talk by Alexis from Texas. She did a Google search and discovered that Alexis from Texas was a white porn star from California. She went to Facebook and expressed her disappointment in the school for allowing this. My friend was devastated.

I was amused by the mistaken identity, sure it would be cleared it up soon. After our conversation, my friend's discomfort and embarrasment lessened.

SNIPER

"You were like a sniper on stage!"

I laughed.

"No! You don't understand! It's like you came out of nowhere! This talk was relevant to all ages and is one of those talks where you can remember it for the rest of your life." After speaking, I was swarmed with people. But this young man looked me in the eye and added, "The way you articulated the scriptures made them very applicable to life!"

A few older ladies tearfully said, "This was just for me! God knew I needed to hear this."

These responses blew my mind. Always, I am shocked at the effect of the words God has given me. Once again, I saw God's Word speak to everyone.

This three-day conference in Des Moines, Iowa, felt overwhelming and anxiety threatened to overtake me. None of these people knew me. I had been invited by the youth pastor who had heard me talk about Lessons for Life at Kids Across America. I was to speak separately to a group of single adults, church congregation, and youth. This was the first time I had ever been invited to speak for a whole weekend to different groups. My first evening was spent with the singles, who sat there all serious. After playing a game, laughing, and writing out questions for me to address, the tension left the room. When I gave my speech on singleness not being a disease, and answered most of their questions, we were like old friends.

Before I spoke, a 30-year-old lady tearfully came to me and shared about the pressure she was under by many people, including her own mom, wondering why she wasn't married yet. She fought depression, believing something must be wrong with her. After my presentation, smiling, she shared with me she had grasped she could choose contentment in her singleness. The joy in her face said she now understood that being content today did not mean eliminating the desire to be married someday. I shared with her she was a daughter of the King, created on purpose, with a purpose and for a purpose (mission). She expressed gratitude for her newfound hope.

I spoke to large diverse groups on three different topics. Lots of people gathered around me after each session, desiring one-on-one time with me. God infused me with a strong energy which carried me through the whole weekend. When it was all over, this speaking opportunity took my confidence to a whole new level.

Several people have asked me again and again how I maintained such a high standard of morality. God showed me clearly that it was because of the ABC's. Accountability, Boundaries, and Courage.

Suddenly, I realized I had always had people in my life to hold me accountable, to hold me responsible for my actions. My experience in college with the football player was my wake up call to set boundaries, creating space around me, like a fence to protect me and my valuables. My fear of rejection taught me how to hold to those boundaries with courage.

BRICKS

I scanned the audience, looking for a volunteer. My eyes kept resting on the same woman, so I called her up. I gave my volunteer a brick to hold.

The brick represented a lie, "I'm unloved."

Women sometimes believe things that are not true, but they hold them anyway. I gave her another brick, then another, yet another, naming all these lies:

"I'm not good enough."

"I'm not enough."

"I'm insecure."

"Hopeless."

"Useless."

The lady whispered to me, "It's getting heavy!"

I quietly told her, "I know."

She said, "I'm not talking about the bricks."

I responded, "I know."

Placing a few more bricks/lies in her hands added more weight, and she began to shake. She whispered, "I'm getting ready to break!"

I told her, "That's okay."

However, she fought so hard to keep holding them. She refused to drop anything, concerned about what the other ladies would think of her. I explained to the audience so many of us carry weight like this and refuse to let anything go. We worry about how others see us. We want no one to see our struggle. But if we don't let go of those bricks—the lies—we'll break.

I asked my audience, "How can we help her?"

They began to shout out encouraging truths, like "You are loved!"

I removed a brick.

Again, someone said, "You are of great worth!"

Another brick gone.

"Your security is in Christ."

Brick gone.

"You are not an accident!"

Brick gone.

As her load lightened, we could see she began to lighten. When I removed the final brick, she broke down, cried, fell into my arms and thanked me over and over.

Later, I was told the entire audience was crying. Friends of hers came to me and asked why I'd picked her.

"I believe the Lord led me directly to her," I said. "It was Spirit led."

Her friends were astounded and said she was bearing a huge load of lies in her life, and this illustration revealed her own freedom to her as well as everyone else. Afterward, she said she'd been seeking a freedom from the Lord all weekend long at this conference. I was the final speaker, and she felt she was doomed if something didn't touch her now. Her direct participation in this message and illustration brought her to a place of finally grasping God's freedom.

I was so pleased to see God moving in her life, but He was also moving in mine. Afterward, with more details about her life and the miracle we witnessed, I was more empowered, certain that God was using me.

AFTERWORD

Each step of my walk has moved me from fear to faith, from hurt to healing, from uncertainty to security and freedom. The length of my journey has brought me to a place of deep trust in God's leading in my life. Experiences that had destructive potential, instead, grew in me new ways of trusting God. As a messenger I am now responsible to pass along all that the Lord has taught me. A gift I gave the girls one year, bore the quote, "Guard it, Use it, Reproduce it," echoes that thought. As the mentors and I speak truth into their lives, they are to guard it by holding their hearts safe from destruction. Using those truths drives them to action, to making positive life choices for themselves. Reproducing it lets them know they now have something worth sharing with others.

If somebody had told me years ago I would be overseeing 91 girls and their mentors, speaking all over the world, and doing intense godly counseling, I would've run as fast as I could the other way. Yet here I am. God is blessing me to the max. Everything has grown one small step at a time. Each step revealed a need I had been uniquely prepared to address, and the blessings just exploded.

I am open to God's leading, trusting Him to continue to use my life to impact the world for His Kingdom. I view the future with a deep fearlessness because of my sincere trust in God. Years ago, Mona Garret, my high school FCA leader, encouraged us by saying, "Put first things first and that is Christ!" This holds true for me still to this day.

PRAYER

Father, as I am looking back over my life, I'm in awe of how You have guided me every step of the way. I see your hand on my life from the beginning. It's clear to me as Psalm 139:13-14 says:

"For You created my inmost being; You knit me together in my mother's womb. I praise You because I am fearfully and wonderfully made; Your works are wonderful, I know that full well."

Lord, I'm most grateful for how Your hand has led me to people and places that I would've never thought or dreamed of. You've taught me so many things that I thought I already knew. When I found myself in places that needed to be shifted, You guided me. When I found myself in situations in which I needed clarity, You sent people, Your people, my way to clear things up. When I thought marriage was the end all, You've shown me there's more and more to life than having a family of my own.

You've kept me—You strategically ordered my steps, not only physically, but spiritually, mentally and emotionally, too. Looking back over my life, I did think early on that I'd be married with kids, but as I trusted You and the call on my life, I'm content. I learned contentment as I followed You and Your leading most of my life. I've learned to trust You, even when I don't understand. I've learned to rest in You even when things weren't clear. I've learned to wait on You, even when others tried to rush me.

Thank You for always reminding me that I'm not alone, that You're with me, and You'll never leave me. Thank You for how You have laid my life out and have helped me to walk in obedience to You and Your guidance. Thank You for loving me in a way that no one could ever love me. Thank You for loving me through Your people, too. Thank you for blessing me with love and support from my family, even when things didn't completely make sense to them. They have loved me hard and well.

You've always been on my side, Lord. Nothing about You has changed—You've always been and always will be my rock.

God, I'm amazed at all You've accomplished in my life. And because I'm still breathing, I know there is more to come.

AMEN!

This is just the last page, but it's not the end of the story.

ABOUT THE AUTHOR

Christian speaker Alexis Ware carries the gospel message to youth and adults worldwide. From her college career as a basketball player for the Texas Tech Lady Raiders to today's middle school hallways, she encourages and challenges people to embrace higher standards.

For more information:

LESSONS For LIFE

lessonsforlife.us

ACKNOWLEDGMENTS

First and foremost, praises and honor to God. God has been TRUTH to me and has modeled TRUTH to me through HIS word. He has blessed my life beyond measures. God has filled my life with so much love, joy, peace and purpose. Thank you, Lord, for allowing me the opportunity to share with the world, all that you have done in my life. I love you God!

I would like to express my sincere and deep gratitude to Darcy Pattison for using her expertise as an author, for giving of herself and time to make sure that this book was written with excellence. I appreciate her for contributing her gifts of writing/publishing etc., to me and her wise words of wisdom along the way. She didn't just teach me how to write a book, but to write a book that people would want to read.

I would also like to extend my deepest thankfulness to Carol Martin for the countless hours we have spent writing this book. Her contribution was invaluable. Through hard work and dedication, Carol was absolutely amazing to work with. I know in my heart that the Lord allowed us to work together to accomplish something that neither one of us had ever dreamed of accomplishing.

I'm extremely grateful for the Lessons for Life Board (Lacy Caldwell, Lynn Pangburn Brunson, Cathy Payne, Tanya Bonham Scott, Angela McElmurry, Shelia Brooks, Missy Cozzens and Kim Parr) for their unwavering guidance. I appreciate them for believing in me even when I didn't believe in myself, for pushing me at times when I didn't think I could take another step. I am thankful for their love and support.

The completion of this book would not have been possible without the Editor's proficiency. The work that she put into this book was astounding!

Texas Tech women's basketball coach, Krista Gerlich was instrumental in providing me with a professional photographer for my book. I could not have asked for a better photographer.

Lessons for Life partners, from the beginning of my ministry, they trusted in what God had called me to do and then took it a step further by contributing their time, resources and finances.

Ministry Family for challenging me to grow deeper in my relationship with Jesus. I thank them for their profound belief in my abilities, allowing me to lead in areas that I would have otherwise not led and their sincere prayers.

I am most honored by my Family and Friends (mentors) for not giving up on me but encouraging me, supporting me, and nurturing me all these years to be the best that I could possibly be.